World of Essential College Vocabulary

BOOK 1

MARGARET ANN RICHEK
Northeastern Illinois University

SUSANNE FRANCINE PICCHI
Joliet Junior College

CENGAGE

Australia • Brazil • Mexico • Singapore • United Kingdom • United States

D0166433

CENGAGE

World of Essential College Vocabulary, Book 1
Margaret Ann Richek, Susanne Francine Picchi

Senior Publisher: Lyn Uhl

Director of Developmental Studies: Annie Todd

Assistant Editor: Elizabeth Rice

Editorial Assistant: Matthew Conte

Media Editor: Amy Gibbons

Marketing Manager: Sophie Teague

Marketing Coordinator: Brittany Blais

Marketing Communications Manager: Courtney Morris

Content Project Manager: Rosemary Winfield

Art Director: Jill Ort

Print Buyer: Betsy Donaghey

Rights Acquisition Specialist: Don Schlotman

Production Service: MPS Limited, a Macmillan Company

Text Designer: Rokusek Design

Cover Designer: Stanton Design

Cover Image: © 1999–2011 Masterfile Corporation. All rights reserved. Endless Media™ (patent pending)

Compositor: MPS Limited, a Macmillan Company

Dedicated to our future: Annabella, Lia, and Chase Picchi and the children descended from Shulim and Manya Geberer

For product information and technology assistance, contact us at
**Cengage Customer & Sales Support, 1-800-354-9706
or support.cengage.com.**

For permission to use material from this text or product, submit all requests online at **www.cengage.com/permissions.**

Library of Congress Control Number: 2011942671

ISBN-13: 978-1-111-83139-4
ISBN-10: 1-111-83139-4

Cengage
20 Channel Street
Boston, MA 02210
USA

Cengage is a leading provider of customized learning solutions with employees residing in nearly 40 different countries and sales in more than 125 countries around the world. Find your local representative at: **www.cengage.com.**

Cengage products are represented in Canada by Nelson Education, Ltd.

To learn more about Cengage platforms and services, register or access your online learning solution, or purchase materials for your course, visit **www.cengage.com.**

Unless otherwise noted, all definitions and pronunciation guides that appear in this book are reproduced by permission from *The American Heritage Dictionary of the English Language*, Fourth Edition. Copyright © 2009 by Houghton Mifflin Harcourt Publishing Company.

Special thanks are due to Marco Parra, Annette Meredith, Joel Meredith, and Teresa Carrillo.

Student photos were taken at Joliet Junior College, in Joliet Illinois. The authors would like to thank the college; JJC photographer Mike O'Brien, photographer Robert E. Potter, III; and students Kelly K. Barrios, Kary Beran, Barbara Bush, Dan (Daniel) Cooper, Adriana Diaz, Shanta Evans, Samec Figueroa, Jonathan Galvan, Jose Eduardo Garcia, Raphael Hernandez, Monica Martinez, Jessica Noyloa, Melissa O'Malley, Tyler Rentfrow, Connor Stenson, Kiara Tremble, DeMotius Turner, Lucas Vanisko, Sarah Welz, Shalisha Wheeler, and Sha'kella Williams.

CONTENTS

TO THE STUDENT

The *World of Essential College Vocabulary, Book 1,* will help you improve your vocabulary. The ability to use precise and varied words in reading, writing, and speaking is important to success. This book teaches 240 key words, and 157 forms derived from them. You will find these words valuable in college, daily life, and your career. The book also presents strategies to help you learn words on your own. The three strategies you will study are: (1) the dictionary, (2) context clues, and (3) word parts (prefixes, roots, and suffixes). You will find these strategies particularly useful when you meet technical words in your chosen field. Finally, to help you review, words are repeated in the chapters that follow the one in which they are taught. An underline (like this) identifies these repeated words.

The book contains four sections. The format for each section is:

- Section introduction: strategy
- First lesson: 20 words; strategy practice
- Second lesson: 20 words; strategy practice
- Third lesson: 20 words; strategy practice
- Review of words and strategy

There are also several reference guides.

- Inside front cover: Parts of speech taught in this book; Pronunciation key
- Inside back cover: Spelling rules for adding suffixes
- Pages 121–123: In-depth guides to dictionary entries and parts of speech

A student website at www.cengagebrain.com provides audio pronunciations, as well as interactive flashcards.

TO THE INSTRUCTOR

This book guides students in vocabulary learning. It can be used independently or with instructor guidance and is suitable for students of many language backgrounds. We chose words based upon several frequency and usage studies, as well as the judgment of many professionals. The books have been extensively piloted in classrooms. The following features are worth noting:

- A two-level format (Books 1 and 2) meets varying student needs.
- A predictable lesson design encourages independent use.
- Ample opportunities for practice foster mastery.
- Words taught are used again in subsequent chapters, and underlined.
- Sound instruction includes accessible definitions, varied practice, inclusion of derivative forms, and the use of words in a timely and entertaining passage.
- Lessons are divided into two parts, which may be taught separately.
- An instructor website at http://login.cengage.com contains a full testing program, PowerPoint presentations, a research database, and other teaching resources. A print manual is available upon request.

Margaret Richek, mrichek@ameritech.net
Susanne Picchi, spicchi@jjc.edu

STRATEGY: THE DICTIONARY

INTRODUCTION

Welcome to the *World of Essential College Vocabulary*, Book 1. This introduction to Section 1 focuses on how to use the dictionary and dictionary websites. Parts of speech are also presented, since they are essential to dictionary use. The dictionary is a wonderful guide to word meaning and use. However, it takes skill to use this tool. For this reason, your book provides some additional resources:

- Short guide to parts of speech (inside front cover)
- Dictionary pronunciation key (inside front cover)
- Expanded guide to parts of speech (pp. 121–122)
- Expanded guide to dictionary entries (p. 123)

PARTS OF SPEECH

Knowing about parts of speech helps you learn and use vocabulary. The words taught in this book are **nouns**, **adjectives**, **verbs**, and **adverbs**. An example sentence shows all of these.

> While she was on a sunny beach, Amy slowly read an extremely long book about justice.

Noun: A **noun** is a person, place, thing, or idea. The sentence above has all four types.

> *Beach* is a place. *Amy* is a person. *Book* is a thing. *Justice* is an idea.

Adjectives: **Adjectives** describe nouns. Look for sunny and long in the example sentence.

> The adjective *sunny* describes *beach*. The adjective *long* describes *book*.

Verbs: **Verbs** indicate an action or a state of being. In the example, was and read are verbs. The verb was is a state of being; it is a form of the verb *to be*. The verb read is an action.

English verbs are complex and have different tenses, including past, present, and future. You may know that the ending *-ed* signals a past tense, as in the word walked. Transitive verbs have direct objects, but intransitive verbs do not. In the example sentence, read is a transitive verb, and its direct object is *book*. However, the verb was is an intransitive verb that does not have a direct object.

Adverbs: **Adverbs** describe verbs, adjectives, and other adverbs. They often end in *-ly*. In the example sentence, slowly and extremely are adverbs. The adverb slowly describes the verb read and extremely describes the adjective long.

THE DICTIONARY

Section 1 of this book gives you practice in dictionary use. You can look up words in a printed dictionary or use an online dictionary. This dictionary entry for *hasty* is taken from an online source. Each part of the entry is labeled.

hast·y 🔊 (hā′stē) KEY ————→ Word and pronunciation

ADJECTIVE: ————————→ Part of speech and word forms
hast·i·er, hast·i·est ————————→

1. Characterized by speed; rapid. See Synonyms at fast.
2. Done or made too quickly to be accurate or wise; ————→ Definitions
   rash: *a hasty decision.*
3. Easily angered; irritable. ————

OTHER FORMS:
hast′i·ly (*Adverb*), hast′i·ness (*Noun*) ————→ Other forms (also called related words, derivatives)

Word and pronunciation: Next to the word are symbols that tell you how to pronounce it. In an online dictionary, the key to these symbols is found by clicking on the symbol KEY. Print dictionaries have keys on each two-page spread. A key is also found on the inside front cover of this book. The key lists a common word that contains each pronunciation symbol. For example, the *a* in *hasty* is pronounced like the *a* in *pay*. A mark like this ′ appears after a syllable that is stressed in speech. Some words have stronger stress marks (′) and weaker stress marks (′). If you click on the sign 🔊, you can hear a word's pronunciation.

Sometimes an entry lists two pronunciations. In this case, the first one is preferred, but the second is acceptable.

Part of speech and word forms: *Hasty* is an adjective, and the comparative word forms for adjectives are given in this entry (*hastier, hastiest*). Entries for nouns list the spelling for the plural form. For verbs, past and present tense endings are given. It is important to remember that some words serve as more than one part of speech.

Definitions: There are three definitions for *hasty*. Which definition would fit in this sentence? "He did such a hasty job on the assignment that he had to do it again"? (The answer is 2.)

The definitions also give you links to synonyms (words that mean the same thing) for *hasty*. Synonyms are listed under *fast* and *impetuous*.

Other forms: These are related words (or derivatives), related to *hasty*, that function as other parts of speech. *Hastily* is an adverb; *hastiness* is a noun.

Houghton Mifflin Harcourt, *The American Heritage Dictionary of the English Language*, 4th ed., © 2009. Reprinted by permission.

VALUABLE WORDS

PART 1: VALUABLE WORDS

arrogant	calamity	jargon	lenient	profound
redundant	spectacular	stringent	turmoil	versatile

In your courses, you must master *jargon* (or technical words). You have probably met some professors who enforce their requirements in a *stringent* (strict) manner and others who are *lenient* (not strict). Whatever your college experience, you will find these words useful.

1. **arrogant** (ăr′ə-gənt) *adjective*
   feeling superior to others

   > The **arrogant** tennis player believed he could defeat any opponent.

   > It is **arrogant** for a club president to schedule events without even asking members.

   arrogance *noun*   The actor showed his *arrogance* when he ignored the director's guidelines.

2. **calamity** (kə-lăm′ĭ-tē) *noun*   **plural: calamities**
   a terrible event; a disaster

   > In 2005, the southeast U.S. suffered the **calamities** of Hurricanes Katrina, Rita, and Wilma.

   > The power outage was a **calamity** for the night ball game.

3. **jargon** (jär′gən) *noun*
   the specialized vocabulary or language of a profession

   > The terms *Acicular Ice, chronoanemoisothermal* diagram, and *Doppler radar* are part of the **jargon** of weather prediction.

   > The law book had so much **jargon** that I couldn't understand it.

4. **lenient** (lē′nē-ənt, lēn′yənt) *adjective*
   not strict or severe

   > We feel that a day in jail is a **lenient** sentence for robbery.

   leniency *noun*   The teacher showed *leniency* in accepting late assignments.

5. **profound** (prə-found′) *adjective*
   very large in influence; strong

   > Einstein's discoveries had a **profound** effect on physics.

   > Because of his **profound** sense of responsibility, the older brother raised his two sisters after their parents died.

   profoundly *adverb*   The great coach *profoundly* influenced players.

an arrogant man

Jargon can be a negative term, referring to overly technical words or sophisticated sounding nonsense.

Profound often refers to ideas or influences, rather than things in the physical world.

6. **redundant (rĭ-dŭn′dənt)** *adjective*
   repetitive; extra

   Little and *small* are **redundant** in the sentence, "He is little and small."

   The firm eliminated three of the five **redundant** mail rooms.

   redundancy *noun*   Airplanes safety systems have *redundancies* that prevent a crash if something fails.   **plural: redundancies**

7. **spectacular (spĕk-tăk′yə-lər)** *adjective*
   very noticeable and impressive

   We had a **spectacular** view from the top of the skyscraper.

   The online game Farmville has been a **spectacular** success.

   spectacularly *adverb*   The fireworks were *spectacularly* beautiful.

8. **stringent (strĭn′jənt)** *adjective*
   strict; having rigid standards

   The city's **stringent** policy forbids smoking both indoors and outside.

   There were **stringent** requirements for the honors program.

   stringency *noun*   The *stringency* of the safety laws reduced accidents.

> The words *stringent* and *lenient* are opposites.

9. **turmoil (tûr′moil′)** *noun*
   extreme trouble and confusion

   The violent revolution threw the country into **turmoil**.

   Her mind was in **turmoil** after her fiancé cancelled the wedding.

10. **versatile (vûr′sə-təl)** *adjective*
    capable of doing many things

    That **versatile** actor can sing, dance, and do acrobatics.

    versatility *noun*   The *versatility* of duct tape allows it to be used as clothing, insect traps, and bandages.

DEFINITIONS: Write the correct word for each meaning.

arrogant	calamity	jargon	lenient	profound
redundant	spectacular	stringent	turmoil	versatile

_____ 1. specialized vocabulary

_____ 2. capable of doing many things

_____ 3. not strict or severe

_____ 4. very impressive and noticeable

_____ 5. repetitive

_____ 6. strict

_____ 7. feeling superior to others

_____ 8. very strong in influence

_____ 9. extreme confusion

_____ 10. a disaster

PART 1 EXERCISES
CONTEXT: ITEMS 1–9: Choose the best answer. ITEM 10: Circle true (T) or false (F).

a. arrogant	b. calamity	c. jargon	d. lenient	e. profound
f. redundant	g. spectacular	h. stringent	i. turmoil	j. versatile

_____ 1. The very ___ rules at work require me to be exactly on time every day.

_____ 2. One "thank you" is enough; it is ___ to offer your thanks many times.

_____ 3. My ___ phone provides access to a date book, e-mail, a contact list, and many apps.

_____ 4. We saw a(n) ___ display of bright red, orange, and yellow autumn leaves.

_____ 5. This book has many ___ ideas that really make you think about the meaning of life.

_____ 6. The ___ parents allowed the teenager to stay out until 3 AM.

_____ 7. The flood was a(n) ___ that destroyed many homes.

_____ 8. A student has to understand lots of medical ___ to have a career in the health sciences.

_____ 9. The ___ young man would only talk to people who were rich and famous.

T   F   10. A city would probably be in *turmoil* after a *calamity*.

DERIVATIONS: Write the correct word form using the choices below.

1. The _____ of FDA demands makes drug approval difficult. (**stringent, stringency**)

2. This paper has many _____. (**redundancy, redundancies**)

3. The officer showed _____ by only giving her a warning for speeding. (**lenient, leniency**)

4. That _____ athlete plays football, basketball, and baseball. (**versatile, versatility**)

5. People dislike him because of his _____. (**arrogance, arrogant**)

6. The price of gold rose _____ last year. (**spectacularly, spectacular**)

FINISH UP: Complete each sentence with a detailed phrase.

1. Because of the *calamity*_____

_____.

2. There was so much *jargon* in the article that _____

_____.

GIVE EXAMPLES: Answer with personal responses.

1. Give an example of something that made a *profound* change in your life, and explain why.

2. Give one way that people react when there is *turmoil* in their lives.

DESCRIPTIONS: Choose the word that these examples best describe.

Example:

___d___   very hard requirements; a dress code that requires men to shave each day; the qualifications to become a doctor
    a. turmoil   **b.** lenient   **c.** jargon   **d.** stringent

_____ 1. I will, I will; Yes, yes; Super, super, super!
    a. redundant   **b.** versatile   **c.** lenient   **d.** jargon

_____ 2. letting people break rules; not sticking to requirements; accepting late papers
    a. lenient   **b.** calamity   **c.** spectacular   **d.** arrogant

_____ 3. Super Bowl halftime show; beautiful mountain view; great rock concert
    a. arrogant   **b.** lenient   **c.** spectacular   **d.** calamity

_____ 4. "You are not as good as me." "I'm too smart for this class." "My children are better than yours."
    a. stringent   **b.** turmoil   **c.** arrogant   **d.** profound

_____ 5. a riot; a cafeteria food fight; a crowd running out of a burning building
    a. turmoil   **b.** redundant   **c.** lenient   **d.** versatile

STRATEGY PRACTICE: Interpreting Dictionary Entries

Read this entry from an online source and answer the questions.

---

en·dorse 🔊 (ĕn-dôrs′) KEY

VERB:

en·dorsed, en·dors·ing, en·dors·es

1. To write one's signature on the back of (a check, for example) as evidence of the legal transfer of its ownership.

2. To place (one's signature), as on a contract, to indicate approval of its contents or terms.

3. To give approval of or support to, especially by public statement; sanction: *endorse a political candidate.* See Synonyms at <u>approve</u>.

OTHER FORMS: **en·dors′a·ble** (*Adjective*), **en·dors′er** or **en·dor′sor** (*Noun*)

_____ 1. How many definitions does *endorse* have in this entry?

_____ 2. What is the part of speech of *endorse*?

_____ 3. Which word in this book's key has the same sound as the first *e* in *endorse*?

_____ 4. What adjective is formed from *endorse*?

_____ 5. Give the number of the definition that fits this sentence: "I *endorse* you for office."

PART 2: MORE VALUABLE WORDS

alter	compel	extravagant	immense	impulsive
methodical	multiple	prediction	thrifty	vivid

This list has two pairs of opposites. To be *thrifty* is to save money; to be *extravagant* is to spend lots of it. *Methodical* people follow an organized system, but *impulsive* people do things suddenly and without planning.

11. alter (ôl′tər) *verb*
     to change
     > She **altered** the pants so they would fit better.
     > The government will **alter** policies for student loans.
     alteration *noun*   The *alterations* in the college schedule were so confusing that many students missed the first day of class.

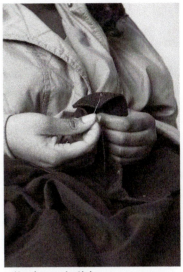

altering clothing

12. compel (kəm-pĕl′) *verb*
     to force
     > The sergeant **compelled** the soldiers to do 200 pushups each day.
     > By law, parents are **compelled** to use car safety seats for children.

13. extravagant (ĭk-străv′ə-gənt) *adjective*
     spending or costing too much money; unreasonably high
     > Hip hop artists often wear **extravagant** jewelry.
     > Despite the **extravagant** claims for vitamin C, research shows that it doesn't prevent colds.
     extravagance *noun*   The diamond ring is an *extravagance*, but I'm worth it!

14. immense (ĭ-mnĕs′) *adjective*
     extremely large
     > The sun is **immense** as compared with the earth.
     > A knowledge of English is an **immense** advantage in business.
     immensity *noun*   We were impressed by the *immensity* of Egypt's pyramids.
     immensely *adverb*   It is *immensely* important to do well on the final exam.

15. impulsive (ĭm-pŭl′sĭv) *adjective*
     sudden and without planning
     > She made an **impulsive** decision to dive into the pool with her clothes on.
     > Their **impulsive** marriage took place after only two dates.
     impulse *noun*   Resist the *impulse* to buy things you can't afford!

Methodical and *impulsive* are opposites.

16. **methodical** (mə-thŏd′ĭ-kəl) *adjective*
systematic and careful
> The **methodical** shopper compared prices on several websites.
> Nurses must be **methodical** in following hospital procedures.

method *noun*   My study *method* helps me learn vocabulary.

Multiple can also mean a whole number you get when you multiply. Since 2 × 3 = 6, the number 6 is a *multiple* of 2.

17. **multiple** (mŭl′tə-pəl) *noun*
many; involving many people, things, or times
> This book has been translated into English **multiple** times.
> The talented actor has received **multiple** awards.

18. **prediction** (prĭ-dĭk′shən) *noun*
something a person thinks will happen in the future
> The U.S. Census Bureau's **prediction** is that the world's human population will be greater than nine billion by 2050.

predict *verb*   Fortune tellers claim they can *predict* the future.

predictable *adjective*   Most fairy tales have *predictable* endings.

Thrifty and *extravagant* are opposites.

19. **thrifty** (thrĭf′tē) *adjective*
careful about spending money; not wasting money
> My **thrifty** mother furnished her house from garage sales.

thrift *noun*   She shows her *thrift* by only shopping at outlet stores.

20. **vivid** (vĭv′ĭd) *adjective*
bright; making a strong impression
> The **vivid** red lights warned of danger on the highway.
> I have **vivid** memories of fishing with my grandfather.

vividness *noun*   The *vividness* of her description makes her a good writer.

DEFINITIONS: Write the correct word for each meaning.

alter	compel	extravagant	immense	impulsive
methodical	multiple	prediction	thrifty	vivid

_____ 1. to force

_____ 2. systematic

_____ 3. careful with money

_____ 4. to change

_____ 5. something a person thinks will happen

_____ 6. spending too much money

_____ 7. done suddenly and without planning

_____ 8. very large

_____ 9. involving many things

_____ 10. bright

PART 2 EXERCISES

CONTEXT: ITEMS 1–9: Choose the best answer. **ITEM 10:** Circle true (T) or false (F).

a. alter	b. compel	c. extravagant	d. immense	e. impulsive
f. methodical	g. multiple	h. prediction	i. thrifty	j. vivid

_____ 1. That essay is perfect, so I don't want you to ___ anything.

_____ 2. In 2005, he made a(n) ___ that housing prices would fall, and it came true in 2008.

_____ 3. I love the ___ Christmas colors of bright red and green.

_____ 4. In an instant, he made a(n) ___ decision to move to Honolulu.

_____ 5. Five thousand dollars is a(n) ___ price to pay for a dress!

_____ 6. I would like you to take this course, but I can't ___ you to take it.

_____ 7. The world's largest animal is the ___ blue whale.

_____ 8. I applied for the scholarship ___ times before I finally got it.

_____ 9. She was so ___ that she even made a schedule for cleaning the house!

T   F   10. A *thrifty* person would be likely to make an *extravagant, impulsive* purchase.

DERIVATIONS: Write the correct word form using the choices below.

1. The word "exhausted" has more _____ than the word "tired." (**vivid, vividness**)

2. The way he sorted laundry was slow but _____. (**methodical, method**)

3. The _____ wedding used up their entire savings. (**extravagant, extravagance**)

4. We need to make some _____ to the furniture. (**alter, alterations**)

5. On an _____, I made an <u>extravagant</u> purchase. (**impulsive, impulse**)

6. The child stared at the _____ dinosaur skeleton. (**immensity, immense**)

FINISH UP: Complete each sentence with a detailed phrase.

1. If I am *compelled* to give up my car, _____

_____.

2. One *prediction* I have about my life ten years from now is that _____

_____.

GIVE EXAMPLES: Answer with personal responses.

1. Give two examples of things that *thrifty* people do.

2. Give an example of something you have done in *multiple* ways.

PASSAGE: Love in Bird Land

Fill in the word from each column's list that fits best.

Column 1 Choices: compel, impulsive, jargon, lenient, profoundly, stringent

Column 2 Choices: alter, extravagant, predicted, redundancy, turmoil, versatile, vivid

Do you put lots of effort into romance? Even if you do, you probably don't even begin to compare to a bird! Thousands of scientific articles, containing lots

of technical (1) _____, have been devoted to the mating habits of these animals.

Researchers find that birds often behave like they are stars in a soap opera. For example, Dr. Luis Baptista studied an *arrogant* white-crowned sparrow that attacked her mate without mercy. The mate seemed to love her, but he could not

(2) _____ her to stay. One day, she ran off with another male. However, the new relationship was also a *calamity*, for in turn, the new "husband" abused her. Still, she stayed with him and raised baby birds.

Was changing her mate a(n)

(3) _____ act, done without any planning and for no reason? Dr. Baptista thought not. The lady bird probably decided that the new mate was stronger, perhaps because he had a superior song.

The singing abilities of male birds

(4) _____ influence the choice of a mate. The melodies they produce are also a(n)

(5) _____ test of physical fitness. Songs good enough to attract a female bird are

immensely difficult to produce and require the male bird to be very strong. Scientists find that when a female wren decides to be unfaithful, she always chooses a male with a better song than her mate.

© Vishnevskiy Vasily/ shutterstock.com

To show how daring and strong they are some male birds are willing to sing while sitting close to the ground, where they are exposed to danger. In one

study, scientists (6) _____ that males who sang from low branches would be chosen more often by females. And that is exactly what they found.

A bird's appearance and dancing skills also help to attract mates. The male peacock has a *spectacular*

display of (7) _____ green and blue feathers. Males attract females by doing a dance to display these feathers. Peacock feathers get even more beautiful as birds get older. This means that more mature "men" attract lots of "women."

Ostriches use makeup to attract mates, although they don't have to waste money by making

(8) _____ purchases at a department store. Instead, glands in their bodies produce a bright orange oil, which they spread on their feathers.

Some males build houses. The bowerbird *methodically* constructs and decorates a nest that he hopes will attract a female.

Of course, birds are not always thinking about

romance. Their (9) _____ songs and calls serve lots of functions. They can warn of danger, identify individual birds, show control of a certain territory, or just be a way of having fun. Bird

songs also can (10) _____ if circumstances change. Not surprisingly, living near cities has made songs shorter and faster.

As you can see, the beautiful songs you hear birds sing have many meanings to their mates and the other birds around them.

Think About the Passage

1. Do female birds appear to be faithful mates? Defend your answer with evidence from the passage.

2. List *multiple* ways from the passage that birds try to attract mates.

MULTIPLE MEANING WORDS; VALUABLE WORDS

PART 1: MULTIPLE MEANING WORDS

blunt	commit	compensate	concrete	convey
effective	hunch	negotiate	recall	staple

Many English words have several meanings. In fact, the word "run" has 93! Can you think of a few? Here are more words with <u>multiple</u> meanings.

1. blunt (blŭnt) *adjective*
   a. not sharp; dull
      The **blunt** blade on the carving knife needs to be sharpened.
   b. overly truthful, often hurting feelings
      Her **blunt** words about my outfit made me change my clothes.
   bluntness *noun*   The press aide's *bluntness* caused problems for the
      president.

2. commit (kə-mĭt′) *verb*
   a. to promise to do something; to take on an obligation
      I can **commit** to volunteering twice a week at the soup kitchen.
   b. to do something illegal or wrong
      The villain in the movie **committed** a murder.
   commitment *noun*   A wedding ring is a symbol of *commitment*.

   Commit has some other meanings. A person may be *committed* to a psychiatric hospital. We may *commit* a password to memory.

3. compensate (kŏm′pən-sāt′) *verb*
   a. to pay for work
      Are you **compensated** well in that job?
   b. to make up for trouble, a loss, or something negative
      He was **compensated** for his hard work by getting an A on the paper.
      Her fine sense of hearing **compensated** for her vision problems.
   compensation *noun*   The *compensation* from insurance covered my loss
      from the theft.

4. concrete
   a. *noun* (kŏn′krēt′) a hard material of sand and stone in cement
      Concrete blocks are often used to construct the walls of buildings.
   b. *adjective* (kn-krēt′) definite, specific, real
      Your paper has lots of ideas, but no **concrete** examples.

   Note these accents:
   CON-crete—noun
   con-CRETE—adjective

5. convey (kən-vā′) *verb*
   a. to bring from one place to another
      Covered wagons **conveyed** settlers across the U.S. wilderness.
   b. to communicate; to express
      A smile generally **conveys** happiness.
   conveyance *noun*   Buses are *conveyances* that hold many people.

6. effective (ĭ-fĕk′tĭv) *adjective*
   a. working well
      Aspirin is **effective** in reducing pain.
   b. starting at a certain time
      Effective January 1, all students must show identification.
   effect *noun* The quality of coaching has an *effect* on how you play.

A *cause* brings about an *effect*.

hunched over, waiting for the ball

7. hunch (hŭnch) *noun*
   a. *verb* to sit or stand with your back and shoulders bent forward
      The little leaguer **hunched** over, waiting for the ball to come his way.
   b. *noun* a feeling that something will happen
      I had a **hunch** my mom wouldn't let me go to the party.

8. negotiate (nĭ-gō′shē-āt′) *verb*
   a. to try to reach agreement
      We **negotiated** for hours before we finalized the contract.
   b. to succeed in doing something difficult
      The expert skier **negotiated** several sharp curves and jumps.
   negotiation *noun* The *negotiation* ended when I bought the car.

Recall can be a noun, as in "Honda issued a *recall* because of unsafe brakes on its cars." The noun *recall* accents the first syllable.

9. recall (rĭ-kôl′) *verb*
   a. to remember
      I **recall** what fun our family reunions used to be.
   b. to call back an item that has problems
      Honda **recalled** five million cars with faulty airbags.

The noun *staple* refers to the small metal piece used to attach papers together.

10. staple (stā′pəl)
    a. *verb* to attach using thin, folded metal
       Please **staple** those pages together.
    b. *noun* a basic item of food or agriculture
       Rice is a **staple** of diets throughout the world.

DEFINITIONS: Write the correct word for each meaning.

blunt	commit	compensate	concrete	convey
effective	hunch	negotiate	recall	staple

_____ 1. a feeling something will happen

_____ 2. a basic food item

_____ 3. to make up for bad effects

_____ 4. overly truthful

_____ 5. working well

_____ 6. to try to reach an agreement

_____ 7. to communicate

_____ 8. definite, specific, real

_____ 9. to call back an item that has problems

_____ 10. to promise to do something

PART 1 EXERCISES

CONTEXT: ITEMS 1–9: Choose the best answer. **ITEM 10:** Circle true (T) or false (F).

a. blunt	b. commit	c. compensate	d. concrete	e. convey
f. effective	g. hunch	h. negotiate	i. recall	j. staple

_____ 1. I met his sister many times, but I can't ___ her name.

_____ 2. Potatoes are a(n) ___ of diets in Peru, and many families eat them daily.

_____ 3. I would like to ___ to attending the conference, but I am just too busy.

_____ 4. I have a(n) ___ that good things are going to happen!

_____ 5. It took several days to ___ the deal because it was hard to get everyone to agree.

_____ 6. Her gentleness and caring will ___ for her lack of experience as a caregiver.

_____ 7. The new policies are ___ as of this week.

_____ 8. Sidewalks are often made from _____.

_____ 9. A limousine will ___ the bride and groom to the church.

T   F   10. A *blunt* manner will help you to *convey* your consideration for the feelings of others.

DERIVATIONS: Write the correct word form using the choices below.

1. We prefer _____ to fighting. **(negotiated, negotiation)**

2. We want equal _____ for equal work. **(compensation, compensate)**

3. When he saw my sister, my friend _____ a message from me. **(conveys, conveyed)**

4. We know she is a nice person, but we object to her _____. **(blunt, bluntness)**

5. Peaceful protest was immensely _____ in winning independence for India. **(effect, effective)**

6. I have a long-term _____ to this project. **(commitment, commits)**

FINISH UP: Complete each sentence with a detailed phrase.

7. One *concrete* suggestion for improving our school experience is _____

_____.

8. Since corn is a *staple* of U.S. agriculture, _____

_____.

GIVE EXAMPLES: Answer with personal responses.

9. Give two examples of things you *recall* from your childhood.

10. Give an example of a *hunch* you had that came true.

DESCRIPTIONS: Choose the word that these examples best describe.

Example:

___a___   **a successful speech; a technique that improves your bowling score; starting on the fifteenth of March**
    a. effective   **b. commit**   **c. convey**   **d. hunch**

_____ 1. successfully stepping across the stones in a pond; talking to your boss and getting a raise; union representatives and management coming to an agreement about working conditions
    a. recall   **b.** commit   **c.** convey   **d.** negotiate

_____ 2. buying flowers from someone who was rude but whose prices were cheap; getting paid; getting multiple days off in return for taking extra responsibilities at work
    a. staple   **b.** effective   **c.** hunch   **d.** compensate

_____ 3. soybeans; cotton; a small piece of metal that attaches two pieces of paper
    a. staple   **b.** effective   **c.** blunt   **d.** commit

_____ 4. a dangerous crib going back to the manufacturer; memorizing a poem; remembering your wedding
    a. effective   **b.** recall   **c.** convey   **d.** hunch

_____ 5. return a text message; a train taking you to work; thanking someone
    a. commit   **b.** blunt   **c.** concrete   **d.** convey

STRATEGY PRACTICE: Choosing the Right Definition

When a word has more than one definition, you must select the one that best fits the sentence. Read each sentence and choose the definition that fits best. The first one is done for you.

compensate
  a. to make a payment; to pay someone who has suffered a loss
  b. to make up for the bad effect of something else

_____ The candidate's qualifications cannot *compensate* for his dishonesty.

_____ 1. The company *compensates* its workers generously.

recall
  a. to remember
  b. to call back an item that has problems

_____ 2. The supermarket *recalled* the eggs that were infected with salmonella.

_____ 3. I can't *recall* where I put my keys.

commit
  a. to pledge to do something; to take an obligation
  b. to do something illegal or wrong
  c. to place in a psychiatric hospital

_____ 4. She swore she had not *committed* the robbery.

_____ 5. The doctor *committed* the depressed man to a facility.

PART 2: VALUABLE WORDS

arbitrary	allocate	deteriorate	devious	inhibit
proverb	regulate	solemn	tedious	variable

You have probably heard some *proverbs* (well-known sayings). "Practice makes perfect" is a *proverb* about the value of doing things over and over, which is sort of *tedious* (long and boring). "To each his own" describes the *variable* (different) nature of human tastes.

11. arbitrary (är′bĭ-trĕr′ē)
    done for no reason; unfair
    > The principal made an **arbitrary** decision to expel one student who was fighting, but to let the other stay in school.

    arbitrarily *adverb*   The judge *arbitrarily* dismissed the case.

12. allocate (ăl′ə-kāt′) *verb*
    to decide to use something for a specific purpose
    > I plan to **allocate** $75 of my weekly salary to a retirement account.
    > You need to **allocate** more time for studying.

    allocation *noun*   Her food stamp *allocation* was reduced.

13. deteriorate (dĭ-tîr′ē-ə-rāt′) *verb*
    to become worse
    > The deserted house **deteriorated** over the years.

    deterioration *noun*   The spreading bed sores caused a *deterioration* of the patient's condition.

14. devious (dē′vē-əs) *adjective*
    cleverly dishonest
    > The **devious** man convinced elderly widows to invest their money with him and then spent the funds on himself.

    deviously *adverb*   They *deviously* hatched a secret plot.

15. inhibit (ĭn-hĭb′ĭt) *verb*
    to prevent something from happening; to slow something down
    > The laughter of her classmates **inhibited** her from making the speech.
    > Storing meat in the refrigerator will **inhibit** the growth of bacteria.

    inhibition *noun*   Forgetting his *inhibitions*, he impulsively began to dance.

    > When we *inhibit* people, we often hold them back through embarrassment.

16. proverb (prŏv′ûrb′) *noun*
    a well-known statement about life
    > One famous **proverb** is "Honesty is the best policy."

    proverbial *adjective*   Her honesty is *proverbial*. (This means that she is famous for her honesty.)

    > Famous *proverbs* include:
    > * Haste makes waste.
    > * When the cat's away, the mice will play.
    > * Waste not, want not.

Sorting sequins by color is a *tedious* task.

17. regulate (rĕg′yə-lāt′) *verb*
    to control, often by having rules
    > The nurse carefully **regulated** the amount of medication that the patient received.
    > Laws **regulate** the number of hours a pilot can fly.

    regulation *noun*   The new *regulation* required students to wear uniforms.

18. solemn (sŏl′əm) *adjective*
    serious in behavior
    > A funeral is a **solemn** occasion.
    > I give you my **solemn** promise to tell the truth.

    solemnity *noun*   The tribute to veterans was conducted with *solemnity*.

19. tedious (tē′dē-əs) *adjective*
    long and boring
    > Sorting sequins by color is a **tedious** task

    tedium *noun*   She relieved the *tedium* of waiting by reading a book.

20. variable (vâr′ē-ə-bəl)
    a. *adjective* changing; different
    > The weather in Chicago is **variable** and may alter from hour to hour.
    b. *noun* something that changes
    > This **variable** can take on different values in the equation.

    vary *verb*   The announcer *varies* his voice to keep listeners interested.

DEFINITIONS: Write the correct word for each meaning.

arbitrary	allocate	deteriorate	devious	inhibit
proverb	regulate	solemn	tedious	variable

_____ 1. long, boring

_____ 2. unfair; done for no reason

_____ 3. to prevent from happening

_____ 4. decide to use for a specific purpose

_____ 5. serious

_____ 6. cleverly dishonest

_____ 7. to become worse

_____ 8. changing

_____ 9. a well-known statement about life

_____ 10. to control

PART 2 EXERCISES

CONTEXT: ITEMS 1–9: Choose the best answer. **ITEM 10:** Circle true (T) or false (F).

a. arbitrary	b. allocate	c. deteriorate	d. devious	e. inhibit
f. proverb	g. regulate	h. solemn	i. tedious	j. variable

_____ 1. "People who live in glass houses shouldn't throw stones" is a famous ___.

_____ 2. Most people find that studying for several hours without a break is ___.

_____ 3. The graduation ceremony was ___ and quiet, but the party afterward was lots of fun.

_____ 4. If the economy starts to ___, it will be harder to find a job.

_____ 5. The fullness of the moon is ___, and changes each night.

_____ 6. Laws that ___ safety require fire alarms in buildings.

_____ 7. The threat of going to prison will ___ people from breaking this law.

_____ 8. I ___ $100 of my monthly salary to savings for a new car.

_____ 9. For no reason, the city made a(n) ___ change in parking policies.

T   F   10. A *devious* person would strictly follow all rules and *regulations*.

DERIVATIONS: Write the correct word form using the choices below.

1. The amount of pollen in the air is a(n) _____ that affects allergies. (**variable, vary**)

2. The bridge was so _____ that I was afraid to cross it. (**deteriorate, deteriorated**)

3. She is the _____ "early bird who catches the worm." (**proverb, proverbial**)

4. The **swearing** in of a U.S. president is a time of great _____. (**solemnity, solemn**)

5. A state _____ requires motorcyclists to wear helmets. (**regulate, regulation**)

6. The parents gave each child a(n) _____ of $200 for books. (**allocate, allocation**)

FINISH UP: Complete each sentence with a detailed phrase.

7. The *devious* businessman _____

_____.

8. It is *tedious* to _____

_____.

GIVE EXAMPLES: Answer with personal responses.

9. Give an example of an *arbitrary* decision.

10. Give two examples of *inhibited* behavior.

PASSAGE: It's Not What We Say, It's What We Do

Fill in the word from each column's list that fits best.

Column 1 Choices: conveyed, deteriorate, effective, hunches, proverb, recall, vary

Column 2 Choices: bluntness, compensate, hunch, recall, negotiating, tedious

Do human beings always use speech to communicate their messages? Actually, no! According to researchers, up to 90% of our communication is

(1) _____ through body language and gestures.

Your posture and gestures are a *concrete* and effective way to get messages across. For example, a person who stands tall is proud. In contrast, a person who *hunches* over is often shy or ashamed. People usually see a firm handshake as a sign of confidence.

Movement is also a(n)

(2) _____ aid to speaking. Studies show that gestures help us to

(3) _____ words if we have forgotten them. When volunteers were asked to keep their hands still, they had lots of trouble bringing words to mind. Gesture is a *staple* of communication, even for blind people who are talking to other blind people.

Some activities, like smiling and crying, are universal to human beings. However, other actions and gestures are *arbitrarily* determined, and may

(4) _____ from culture to culture.

In most countries, for example, people nod their heads up and down to indicate "yes," and from side to side to indicate "no." But in Sri Lanka and Bulgaria, up and down means "no," and side to side means "yes." Communication between a Bulgarian and a

Canadian might (5) _____ rapidly into a calamity because they just couldn't understand the nods that signal yes and no!

Some cultures encourage closeness and touching. In Brazil, even official conferences end with kisses.

Other cultures are more *inhibited*. Japan has a very formal routine, in which meetings often

begin and end with bows. The depth of the bow is *variable* and is highly *regulated*. It would take

months of (6) _____ study for a visitor to Japan to master how to bow correctly. In the meantime, experts recommend that if you are not familiar with these customs, simply make a small

bow. This will (7) _____ for your lack of knowledge, because people will realize that you are trying.

Another thing to remember, especially if you

are (8) _____ a contract, is never to say "no." Instead, you should say "Yes, but . . . ." Being too direct is not good because

(9) _____ is considered rude in Japanese culture.

Many people in the U.S. and Canada make the sign for OK with their thumb and finger. However, this is considered very rude in Japan, as well as in Austria, France, and some parts of South America. In Thailand and Saudi Arabia, it is considered very bad manners to show the soles of your feet.

© Stephen Coburn/shutterstock.com

As these examples show, it may be very difficult to alter your behavior so that you can effectively *negotiate* in other cultures.

If you have a(n) (10) _____ that you are doing something wrong, simply try to be still!

Think About the Passage

1. Give one example of a gesture whose meaning *varies* from country to country, and one that does not.

2. Give an example of an error you could *commit* using body language in another country, and explain why.

VERB AND NOUN WORDS; VALUABLE WORDS

PART 1: VERB AND NOUN WORDS

ally	attribute	compress	crusade	escort
fracture	lure	monitor	taunt	venture

Many English words are both verbs and nouns. For example, we can *walk* (verb) or we can take a *walk* (noun). This section presents more difficult words that serve as both parts of speech.

1. ally
   a. *verb* to agree to cooperate for a common cause (ə-lī′)
      Great Britain and the United States were **allied** in World War II.
   b. *noun* a person or group that cooperates with another (ăl′ī)
      The Senator and his **ally** worked to get health care reform passed.
   alliance *noun*   Four business associations formed an *alliance* to lower taxes.

> The *y* in *ally* changes to *i* in forms like *allies*, *allied*, and *alliance*.

2. attribute
   a. *verb* to identify as a cause (ə-trĭb′yōōt)
      I **attribute** my success to hard work.
   b. *noun* an ability or characteristic (ăt′rə-byōōt′)
      The ability to work hard is one of my most important **attributes.**

> Note these changes in stress:
>
> | Verb | Noun |
> |---|---|
> | al-LY | AL-ly |
> | a-TRIB-ute | A-trib-ute |
> | com-PRESS | COM-press |
> | es-CORT | ES-cort |

3. compress
   a. *verb* to make smaller, often by pressing together (kəm-prĕs′)
      You can **compress** a basketball by squeezing air out of it.
      The program **compressed** computer files so they could be e-mailed.
   b. *noun* a pad applied with pressure (kŏm′prĕs′)
      If you hold down the **compress,** the blood flow will stop.
   compression *noun*   Poor posture caused *compression* of a nerve in his back.

compressing a basketball

© Robert Erving Potter III

4. crusade (krōō-sād′)
   a. *noun* a dedicated movement that works for a cause
      MADD's **crusade** against drunk driving has helped to change laws.
   b. *verb* To work for a cause with dedication
      Martin Luther King **crusaded** for Civil Rights.
   crusader *noun*   The *crusader* fought for a fair criminal justice system.

> In the original *Crusades*, almost 1,000 years ago, European soldiers attempted to capture the city of Jerusalem.

5. escort
   a. *noun* a person who goes somewhere with another (ĕs′kôrt′)
      My mom was an **escort** for the class trip to Washington D.C.
   b. *verb* to go with someone (ĭ-skôrt′)
      I **escorted** my husband to his doctor's appointment.

6. fracture (frăk′chər)
   a. *noun* a break, especially a crack
      The gymnast's hip **fracture** ended her Olympic hopes.
   b. *verb* to break; to break apart
      The force of the storm **fractured** the bridge in several places.

7. lure (lo͞or)
   a. *noun* something that attracts and tempts
      The **lure** of free video game consoles brought people into the store.
   b. *verb* to tempt or attract in a deceiving way
      False promises **lured** him into accepting the job.

> A *lure* is something that tricks a fish into biting. One example is a worm on the end of a fish hook. In the same way, any type of *lure* is a promise that is often a trap.

8. monitor (mŏn′ĭ-tər)
   a. *noun* a person or thing that watches and checks
      The electronic **monitor** gave information about the patient's pulse.
      Monitors from the U.N. reported on elections in Uganda.
   b. *verb* to watch and check
      Scientists are **monitoring** the effects of lion fish on ocean reefs.

> A *monitor* can also be a screen that shows pictures or data.

9. taunt (tônt)
   a. *verb* to say cruel things to someone
      The boys **taunted** the tall girl by shouting, "Beanpole!"
   b. *noun* A cruel or mocking statement
      "Go home, oldie," was the **taunt** shouted at the senior citizen.

10. venture (vĕn′chər)
    a. *noun* an activity that requires risk
       It took millions of dollars to fund the business **venture.**
       Many people have died in mountain climbing **ventures.**
    b. *verb* to do something that is risky
       She **ventured** into the old barn despite her fear it would collapse.

DEFINITIONS: Write the correct word for each meaning.

ally	attribute	compress	crusade	escort
fracture	lure	monitor	taunt	venture

_____ 1. someone who cooperates with you

_____ 2. a dedicated movement

_____ 3. to say cruel things

_____ 4. to make smaller

_____ 5. to go with someone

_____ 6. an activity that requires risk

_____ 7. to break

_____ 8. an ability or characteristic

_____ 9. to watch and check

_____ 10. to tempt or attract

PART 1 EXERCISES

CONTEXT: ITEMS 1–9: Choose the best answer. **ITEM 10:** Circle true (T) or false (F).

a. ally	b. attribute	c. compress	d. crusade	e. escort
f. fracture	g. lure	h. monitor	i. taunt	j. venture

_____ 1. You need to ___ your redundant fifteen minute speech into five minutes.

_____ 2. I hope you didn't ___ a bone in the car accident.

_____ 3. I can't ___ you to the senior prom unless I pay an extravagant price for a tuxedo.

_____ 4. My ___ and I planned our strategy for defeating the enemy.

_____ 5. The security guards always ___ this dangerous area by video.

_____ 6. I ___ my success to the efforts my mother made to keep me in school.

_____ 7. After his son died of AIDS, he went on a(n) ___ to get better treatment for the disease.

_____ 8. You can ___ me by insulting me, but don't try to start a physical fight!

_____ 9. He tried to ___ me into the gambling casino, but I resisted temptation.

T   F   10. If you invest money into a business *venture*, it is wise to *monitor* how it is spent.

DERIVATIONS: Write the correct word form using the choices below.

1. The three countries formed an _____. (**allies, alliance**)

2. Our _____ is profoundly committed to working for peace. (**crusade, crusader**)

3. My _____ in China also served as a translator. (**escort, escorted**)

4. The Secret Service _____ the vice president's safety. (**monitors, monitor**)

5. Terrible fights within management _____ the company's leadership. (**fracturing, fractured**)

6. Despite my fear, I _____ into the dark cave. (**venturing, ventured**)

FINISH UP: Complete each sentence with a detailed phrase.

7. We can *compress* an aluminum can by _____

_____.

8. My best *attribute* is _____

_____.

GIVE EXAMPLES: Answer with personal responses.

9. Give an example of a way to *lure* people into buying something they can't afford.

10. Give two examples of how you would feel if you were *taunted*.

DESCRIPTIONS: Choose the word that these examples best describe.

Example:

____d____   vase with a crack; a split branch; a broken toe
     a. attribute   **b. crusade**   **c. monitor**   **d. fracture**

_____ 1. nurse <u>regulates</u> patient responses every ten minutes; cleanliness of water is tested each day; every six months, inspectors make certain the elevators are safe
     a. monitor   b. escort   c. fracture   d. attribute

_____ 2. "Hi, ugly!"; "Can't do anything right, can you?"; "Hey, even your mother couldn't love you!"
     a. ally   b. lure   c. taunt   d. venture

_____ 3. starting a pizza restaurant; going into wild forest alone; rafting on a dangerous river
     a. venture   b. compress   c. crusade   d. fracture

_____ 4. country that fights on your side; person who cooperates with you; two senators who try to pass a law
     a. lure   b. escort   c. ally   d. attribute

_____ 5. baiting a trap for a bear; false promises given by a salesman; promising a salary but not paying it
     a. lure   b. compress   c. venture   d. monitor

STRATEGY PRACTICE: Identifying Nouns and Verbs

Read the sentences below and determine whether the word in italics is used as a *noun* or *verb*.

_____ 1. You can *taunt* me, but you will not hurt my feelings.

_____ 2. I have a <u>hunch</u> you want me to respond to your *taunts*, but I won't.

_____ 3. Her aunt was her *escort* at her college interview.

_____ 4. Children must be *escorted* by a responsible adult.

_____ 5. My *fracture* took a long time to heal.

_____ 6. Because of a *fracture* in the club's leadership, many members withdrew.

_____ 7. The experts *attribute* that <u>spectacular</u> painting to Picasso.

_____ 8. Patience is an important *attribute*.

_____ 9. I want to *crusade* for children's rights.

_____ 10. She *crusaded* for the cause she believed in.

PART 2—VALUABLE WORDS

animosity	bizarre	dilapidated	distort	endorse
feasible	initiate	prevalent	sinister	surplus

Have you heard of a *feasible* (workable) plan? Are cell phones *prevalent* (widespread) at school? Do some people you know wear *bizarre* (strange) clothes? These words describe situations that people encounter frequently.

11. animosity (ăn′ə-mŏs′ĭ-tē) *noun*
    hatred; strong dislike

    The strike led to **animosity** between workers and their boss.

12. bizarre (bĭ-zär′) *adjective*
    very strange and unusual

    We knew Grandma's mind was not functioning well when she started doing **bizarre** things like taking baths in apple juice.

> Both *animosity* and *bizarre* are very strong words.

13. dilapidated (dĭ-lăp′ĭ-dā′tĭd) *adjective*
    needing repair; run down

    The **dilapidated** front porch should be cleaned and painted.

    dilapidation *noun*   Peeling paint and exposed electrical wires showed the school's *dilapidation*.

> *Dilapidated* generally refers to buildings.

14. distort (dĭ-stôrt′) *verb*
    a. to twist out of shape

    Artists like Salvador Dali **distorted** objects into <u>bizarre</u> shapes.

    b. to twist or change meaning

    The summary **distorted** the conclusions of the report.

    The nosy neighbor **distorted** the meeting between the man and the woman to make it seem like a love affair.

a *distorted* object

© francesco riccardo iacomino/shutterstock.com

15. endorse (ĕn-dôrs′) *verb*
    a. to make a public statement of support

    The teachers' union **endorsed** a Democrat for president.

    b. to transfer ownership of a check by signing a name on the back.

    If I **endorse** a check made out to me, and I give it to my mother, she will be able to cash it.

    endorsement *noun*   We want the dean's *endorsement* of our proposal.

16. feasible (fē′zə-bəl) *adjective*
    possible; likely to succeed

    Your plan for finishing college while working is **feasible**.

    The development of natural gas resources may make it **feasible** for the U.S. to meet all of its own energy needs.

    feasibility *noun*   Officials studied the *feasibility* of building a new highway.

17. initiate (ĭ-nĭsh′ē-āt′) *verb*
    to start; to admit as a member

    > The Securities and Exchange Commission **initiated** an investigation into the illegal trading of stocks.

    > Perry was **initiated** into the Collectors Club of Chicago.

    initiation *noun* The party for students was a nice *initiation* into college.

18. prevalent (prĕv′ə-lənt) *adjective*
    very common; widespread

    > We were shocked at how **prevalent** cyber bullying has become.

    > Cholera can become **prevalent** in places with unclean water.

    prevalence *noun* Because of the *prevalence* of crime, my mother wanted me home before dark.

19. sinister (sĭn′ĭ-stər) *adjective*
    threatening harm or evil

    > We trembled with fear as the **sinister** man in the black hood drew close to us.

    > The drink has the **sinister** nickname of "blackout in a can," so I can't imagine it is good for you.

Like many nouns, *surplus* can be used as an adjective, as in *surplus clothing*.

20. surplus (sûr′pləs) *noun*   plural: **surpluses**
    extra things; more than is needed

    > We were delighted to see a **surplus** of cash in our account.

    > The settlers stored the **surplus** of wheat in a granary.

DEFINITIONS: Write the correct word for each meaning.

| animosity | bizarre | dilapidated | distort | endorse |
| feasible | initiate | prevalent | sinister | surplus |

_____ 1. to twist out of shape

_____ 2. needing repair

_____ 3. extra things

_____ 4. very common; widespread

_____ 5. to make a statement of support

_____ 6. strong dislike

_____ 7. to start

_____ 8. possible; likely to succeed

_____ 9. very strange

_____ 10. threatening evil

PART 2 EXERCISES

CONTEXT: ITEMS 1–9: Choose the best answer. **ITEM 10:** Circle true (T) or false (F).

a. animosity	b. bizarre	c. dilapidated	d. distort	e. endorse
f. feasible	g. initiate	h. prevalent	i. sinister	j. surplus

_____ 1. It is not ___ for my sick mother to travel, so we will all go to visit her.

_____ 2. Sardine ice cream would be considered a(n) ___ flavor.

_____ 3. If I ___ the check over to you, you can get the money for it.

_____ 4. There is a(n) ___ of houses for sale, so we have many choices.

_____ 5. The university will ___ three people into an honors society today.

_____ 6. When a lack of rain caused the crops to fail, hunger became ___ in the area.

_____ 7. The ___ look on the man's face suggested that he might want to harm us.

_____ 8. Journalists try not to ___ the facts, for they want to write truthful reports.

_____ 9. It is time to tear down this ___ old house.

T   F   10. *Animosity* is *prevalent* between people who are enemies.

DERIVATIONS: Write the correct word form using the choices below.

1. We will _____ new policies. (**initiate, initiating**)

2. The NBA star _____ the brand of sneakers. (**endorsed, endorsement**)

3. The _____ of the building lowers its value. (**dilapidated, dilapidation**)

4. Teachers complained about the _____ of texting in class. (**prevalent, prevalence**)

5. We are investigating the _____ of your plan. (**feasible, feasibility**)

6. The report had been _____ by altering the conclusions. (**distorted, distort**)

FINISH UP: Complete each sentence with a detailed phrase.

7. We felt a *sinister* presence in the room when _____

_____.

8. Because of my *animosity* toward the man, _____

_____.

GIVE EXAMPLES: Answer with personal responses.

9. Give an example of a *bizarre* situation that you have seen or read about.

10. What would a thrifty person do with a *surplus* of food?

PASSAGE: From Poison to Perfect: A History of the Potato

Fill in the word from each column's list that fits best.

Column 1 Choices: attributed, distorted, feasible, ally, surpluses, ventured

Column 2 Choices: bizarre, crusade, lured, monitors, prevalent, taunted

High up in the mountains of Bolivia and Peru, 7,000 years ago, humans began to eat a remarkable food: the potato. Rich sources of vitamins B, C, D, and iron can be *attributed* to this small tuber. In fact, it gives the most food value, per acre, of any plant. And it can be grown almost anywhere. The potato made

it (1) _____ for South Americans to live in cold, mountainous areas with poor soil quality. Ancient Incas took potatoes on trips,

stored (2) _____ in case of hard times, and even included them in prayers.

   When European explorers

(3) _____ into Peru, they discovered the small plant and brought it back home. Unfortunately, potatoes did not have an easy *initiation* into Europe. People found it strange that the food grew underground. They also felt that the potato had a *bizarre* appearance, since many looked like

(4) _____ human heads.

People mistakenly (5) _____ all sorts of diseases to eating potatoes.

   But in *dilapidated* huts across Europe, poor peasants needed the nutrition that the potato provided. Wishing to feed his people, German King Frederick William <u>compelled</u> all peasants in his kingdom to plant potatoes. He actually threatened

to cut off the noses and ears of those who would not follow his orders! Peter the Great, king of Russia, also had to encourage potato growing by force.

In France, Antoine-Augustin Parmentier went on

a one-man (6) _____ to spread the potato's popularity. He planted several acres, and sent guards to protect them. Then, one day, he deliberately left the field unprotected. Assuming that they must be valuable, farmers were

(7) _____ into stealing some potatoes and planting them. Parmentier also engaged King Louis XVI as an *ally.* The king *endorsed* the potato and persuaded his glamorous wife, Marie Antoinette, to wear potato flowers in her hair.

   People in Ireland came to rely on the crop—until the <u>calamity</u> of the Irish Potato Famine. In 1845, potatoes rotted from a disease, and over a million people died of starvation. The smell of sour potatoes filled the air. A cure for the disease was not discovered until forty years later.

   Modern Americans now eat an average of 140 pounds of potatoes each year—much of it in the form of potato chips. Some

(8) _____ report that 18 million pounds are eaten during the Super Bowl!

   The potato is everywhere; it has become

(9) _____ in our culture. Mr. Potato Head is a well-known toy, the Mashed Potato is a song and dance, and a person who watches TV all day is called a "couch potato."

   The potato is also used in insults. In 2003, an Irish employee asked why his salary had been cut.

In response, his boss (10) _____ him by saying, "If you don't like it, you can go back to Ireland and pick potatoes." The employee brought a lawsuit, and was awarded $500,000!

Think About the Passage

1. Give two examples of how people were tricked into or forced to grow and eat potatoes.

2. Which incident in this passage seems the most *bizarre* to you?

This section will help you review words from lessons 1, 2, and 3. It will also provide practice in the strategy of using the dictionary.

DEFINITIONS: Fill in the letter that matches the definition of each word.

_____	1. solemn	a. cleverly dishonest
_____	2. devious	b. not sharp
_____	3. extravagant	c. spending too much money
_____	4. dilapidated	d. a risky or difficult activity
_____	5. staple	e. needing repair
_____	6. stringent	f. strict
_____	7. venture	g. a wise and experienced person
_____	8. blunt	h. to force
_____	9. jargon	i. a major, basic item of food
_____	10. crusade	j. serious
		k. a dedicated movement that works for a cause
		l. the specialized vocabulary of a profession

DERIVATIONS: Write the correct word form using the choices below.

1. Her _____ enabled the actor to play different roles.
   (**versatile, versatility**)

2. The _____ of washing dishes bored me to tears.
   (**tedious, tedium**)

3. Students should try to write without _____.
   (**redundant, redundancy**)

4. When she fell last week, she _____ her arm.
   (**fractured, fracture**)

5. I hope you will _____ the candidate I support.
   (**endorse, endorsement**)

6. School districts receive an _____ of funds for each special education student they serve. (**allocate, allocation**)

7. Many things are _____ me from expressing my true emotions. (**inhibiting, inhibition**)

CONTEXT: Write the letter of the word that best completes each sentence. Use each choice only once.

a. ally	b. calamity	c. commit	d. compensate
e. distort	f. effective	g. escort	h. feasible
i. profound	j. prediction	k. regulate	l. sinister

_____ 1. A(n) ___ took my disabled grandfather to the community center.

_____ 2. In the movie, the ___ criminals plotted to destroy the world.

_____ 3. Great Britain was the ___ of the U.S. in World War II, and the two countries fought together to defeat the Nazis.

_____ 4. If it is financially ___, I will buy a new computer.

_____ 5. My teacher's ___ is that I will get an A on tomorrow's test.

_____ 6. Your ___ comments reveal how deeply you have thought about this issue.

_____ 7. The fire that destroyed our house was a(n) ___ for my family.

_____ 8. The new prices are ___ from today until Christmas.

_____ 9. I will ___ for being late to my job by working an hour longer.

_____ 10. I would like to ___ to helping you out, but I don't have the time right now.

PASSAGE: Is It Legal? A History of Clothing

Fill in the word from each column's list that fits best.

Column 1 Choices: attributes, compelled, conveyed, dilapidated, distort, immense, proverb, vivid

Column 2 Choices: arrogant, bizarre, initiate, lenient, monitored, surplus, thrift, turmoil

An Irish (1) _____ states that "Clothes make the man." In fact, most of us put effort into choosing what we wear. Today we can dress as we please. But for hundreds of years, clothing was *regulated* by laws.

In ancient Rome, purple was the color of power. Perhaps this was because an expensive dye named

Tyrian resulted in a very (2) _____ shade that made the color bright and attractive. Only emperors could wear a solid purple cloak. Nobles were allowed to wear purple stripes, and the number

of stripes (3) _____ messages about their ranks.

Europeans in the Middle Ages (1500 to 500 years ago) thought that colors had certain

(4) _____, so meaning was assigned to them. Red, the color of blood, was considered manly. Blue was a soft color, meant for women. Yellow meant cowardly.

Other customs from the Middle Ages also seem

strange today. Women would (5) _____ their appearance by wearing padding to make their stomachs look larger! Toward the end of this period, men started to wear a shirt called a tunic. Instead of pants, they clothed themselves from the feet to the waist with tight-fitting hose. This allowed them to show off their legs. Men also loved jewelry, and they

spent (6) _____ fortunes buying *spectacular* necklaces and earrings.

Some things went in and out of fashion. At one time, men in France grew beards and twisted them into all sorts of fantastic shapes and curls. But then a priest gave a sermon saying that men

should be (7) _____ to get rid of beards. To make his point, he grabbed some beards and cut them off! This started a trend of clean-shaven faces.

In the 1500s, England's Queen Elizabeth feared that nobles were going into debt buying *extravagant* clothes. She wanted to encourage

(8) _____ by limiting what they could buy. She also decided that people needed to buy more English wool, because there was a(n)

(9) _____. So she passed laws forbidding the English to wear wool that was produced outside of the country.

To most of us, the laws about clothing seem so strange that we consider them to be

(10) _____. But to kings and queens, they seemed perfectly logical. Rulers feared that fine clothes might make people

(11) _____ and that this could lead to revolts. They also feared that social

(12) _____ and violence might result if people forgot their place in the world.

Laws *regulating* clothes were quite *stringent*. Violating them meant a person was committing a crime and could be put in prison. Some laws even had death as a punishment. But in practice, clothing was not always closely

(13) _____. People who wore forbidden clothing were not punished because officials tended to be

(14) _____. Still, it is fun to imagine a handsome young man, showing off his well-shaped legs, being dragged to prison for wearing a purple cloak!

© Zadiroka/shutterstock.com

STRATEGY REVIEW: Read the dictionary entry and answer the questions below.

---

re·coil (rĭ-koil′) KEY

VERB:
re·coiled, re·coil·ing, re·coils

1. To spring back, as upon firing.

2. To shrink back, as in fear.

3. To fall back; return: *"Violence does, in truth, recoil upon the violent."* *(Arthur Conan Doyle).*

NOUN:

1. The backward action of a firearm upon firing.

2. The act or state of recoiling; reaction.

OTHER FORMS:
re·coil′er *(Noun)*

_____ 1. What two parts of speech does *recoil* function as?

_____ 2. What word in the pronunciation key has a vowel pronounced like the *e* in *recoil?* (Use the front inside cover of your book to answer.)

_____ 3. Which syllable of *recoil* is accented?

_____ 4. What noun is derived from *recoil?*

_____ 5. What is the past tense form of *recoil?*

_____ 6. What do you get on a dictionary website if you click on KEY?

Give the part of speech and the number of the definition that fits these sentences.

_____ 7. We *recoiled* from the sight of so much blood.

_____ 8. The gun *recoiled* in my hand.

_____ 9. Evil deeds often *recoil* on those who have committed wrong.

_____ 10. The *recoil* of the gun may have injured my arm.

Houghton Mifflin Harcourt, *The American Heritage Dictionary of the English Language,* 4th ed., © 2009. Reprinted by permission.

STRATEGY: CONTEXT CLUES

INTRODUCTION

Section 2 of this book teaches you to use *context clues*. *Context clues* are hints to meaning that appear in a sentence with an unknown word. You probably already use context clues, although you may not realize it. If a word has many meanings, context clues allow you to choose the one that fits in a particular sentence. The word "take" has over 50 meanings. Can you match the correct meaning for the sentences below?

Sentences	Meanings
1. Will you *take* my hand?	a. swallow
2. I will *take* those pills with water.	b. hold
3. Don't let the thief *take* your purse.	c. steal

The answers are 1—b; 2—a; 3—c

    Using context clues will save you time, for you can make intelligent guesses about unknown words. This allows you to keep reading without immediately going to a dictionary. However, you should be sure to check the dictionary (or dictionary website) meaning later because context clues are not perfect. The clues often give you only a general sense of a word's meaning, rather than a full meaning. In addition, sometimes there are not many clues in a sentence. In this sentence, the context around the word *livid* is not helpful:

    He was *livid*.

Still, context clues are often useful. In fact, research shows that people learn most of their vocabulary from using context. Three types of clues are:

(1) clues of substitution,
(2) clues of definition,
(3) clues of opposition.

CONTEXT CLUES OF SUBSTITUTION

In context clues of *substitution*, we substitute a word or phrase that makes sense for an unknown word in a sentence. That word (or phrase) is a probable meaning for the unknown word. Here are a few examples:

    We realized how *livid* he was when he screamed at us. (*Livid* means "angry.")
    We could see to the bottom of the *limpid* lake. (*Limpid* means "clear.")
    Smoke *emanated* from a building that was on fire. (*Emanated* means "came out.")

Can you figure out what these words mean in the sentence below?

1. I can't *fathom* why you did such a stupid thing.
2. The water *permeated* the sponge.

The answers are 1. understand;   2. soaked through

CONTEXT CLUES OF DEFINITION

In a *context clue of definition*, the word is defined for you. Definition clues are often used in textbooks, which contain many technical meanings. There are several types of definition clues.

> *Direct Definition*: A definition is simply given for a word. Look for the underlined words below.
> > The fly is *minuscule*, <u>which is to say, very small</u>. (*Minuscule* is "very small.")
> > Don't *impel* us <u>by ordering us to do this</u>. (*Impel* means "ordering" or "forcing.")
> *Commas, Dashes, Parentheses*: These often signal clues of definition.
> > We ate cobia <u>— a type of fish —</u> for dinner. (*Cobia* is a fish.)
> > Her *limbic system*, <u>part of the brain,</u> was damaged. (*Limbic system* is "part of the brain.")
> > The *halcyon* <u>(calm)</u> days were delightful. (*Halcyon* means "calm.")
> *Agreement Words*: Words that help to define meaning include *and, also, likewise, similarly,* and *or.*
> > We saw <u>robins, sparrows, and</u> *avocets*. (The *and* hints that *avocets* are birds.)
> > He <u>won</u> the first race, <u>likewise</u> he *prevailed* in the second. (*Prevailed* means "won.")
> > She *embellished*, <u>or added decorations</u>, to the costume. (*Embellished* means decorated.)

See if you can figure out what the words in italics mean in the sentences below:

1. The *clamor* from next door was terrible, and so was the noise from above.
2. The king's *dominion*, or lands he ruled, went from the sea to the mountains.

Answers: 1. noise   2. lands that are ruled; kingdom

CONTEXT CLUES OF OPPOSITION

In a *context clue of opposition*, a word is defined by an opposite. Here are some clue types.

> *No, not*: These common words show that an opposite meaning is called for.
> > They are <u>not friends</u>, and are, in fact, *antagonists*. (*Antagonists* means *enemies*, the opposite of friends.)
> *Negative words*: These include *but, although, merely, barely, never, rarely, rather than, unless,* and *without.*
> > He <u>has had enough to eat, but</u> I am *ravenous*. (*Ravenous* means hungry.)
> > You are <u>experienced</u> in chess; I am <u>merely</u> a *novice*. (*Novice* means beginner.)
> > <u>Although one place is easily seen</u>, the <u>other</u> is *secluded*. (*Secluded* means hidden from view.)

See if you can figure out what the words in italics mean in the sentences below:

1. Martin was skillful at doing housework, but Martina was *inept*.
2. The man was *impecunious*, and many of his friends were also without money.

Answers: 1. not skillful   2. without money; broke

COMPOUND WORDS; VALUABLE WORDS

PART 1: COMPOUND WORDS

backlog	brainwash	downcast	downturn	foresight
insight	ironclad	outrage	taskmaster	trailblazer

The words in this section are compounds, made up of two words placed together. The smaller words give clues to the meaning of the larger word. For example, to *brainwash* means to force people to believe something new. This is just as if the old ideas in their brains had been washed away, and new ideas had replaced them.

1. backlog (băk′lŏg′) *noun* (back + log)
   a large amount of unfinished work or things not done
   > Heavy snow at the airport caused a **backlog** of delayed flights.
   > There was a seven-month **backlog** in processing insurance claims.

2. brainwash (brān′wŏsh′) *verb* (brain + wash)
   to force someone to believe something
   > In year after year of school, the dictator <u>methodically</u> **brainwashed** children into spying on their parents.

3. downcast (doun′kăst′) *adjective* (down + cast)
   a. sad; depressed
   > My friend seemed **downcast** after breaking up with his girlfriend.
   b. pointing downward
   > The child's **downcast** head showed he was ashamed.

4. downturn (doun′tûrn′) *noun* (down + turn)
   a drop; becoming worse
   > A **downturn** in business activity makes it harder for people to get jobs.
   > The town experienced an **economic** downturn after the large factory closed.
   > A sudden loss of weight can often indicate a **downturn** in a patient's health.

5. foresight (fôr′sīt′) *noun* (fore + sight) (*Fore* means *before.*)
   the ability to predict and plan for the future
   > People live comfortably in retirement if they have the **foresight** to save while they are working.
   > The developer had the **foresight** to realize that the empty field could be turned into a successful shopping center.

6. insight (ĭn′sīt′) *noun* (in + sight)
   deep and clear understanding
   > Knowing about someone's childhood often gives **insight** into his personality <u>attributes</u> and behavior.
   insightful *adjective* After reading that *insightful* article, I understand why the country needs tax reform.

Brainwash is a negative word, suggesting long and systematic forcing of new beliefs. Often, these beliefs seem wrong to others.

© grafica/shutterstock.com

a downcast man

The word *down* suggests something negative in both *downcast* and *downturn*.

In the late 1800s, ships covered, or "*clad*," in *iron*, were considered very strong.

7. ironclad (ī′ərn-klăd′) *adjective* (**iron + clad**)
   unchangeable; firm
   > I will loan you the money if I have an **ironclad** guarantee that you will pay me back.
   > There was an **ironclad** rule that missing a game would get you kicked off the team.

8. outrage (out′rāj′) (**out + rage**)
   a. *verb* to shock and anger
   > The U.N. official was **outraged** at the killing of innocent people.
   b. *noun* something that shocks and angers
   > It is an **outrage** that the rich woman gets government food stamps.
   outrageous *adjective* It is *outrageous* that the bride was late to her own wedding.

9. taskmaster (tăsk′măs′tər) *noun* (**task + master**)
   a person demanding hard work from others
   > The film director was a **taskmaster,** who insisted on shooting scenes <u>multiple</u> times before he was satisfied.

10. trailblazer (trāl′blā′zər) *noun* (**trail + blazer**)
    a pioneer; a person who does new things
    > In the early 1800s, the **trailblazer** led his family to the frontier in Iowa.
    > Physicist Albert Einstein was a **trailblazer** who developed the concept of relativity.

DEFINITIONS: Write the correct word for each meaning.

backlog	brainwash	downcast	downturn	foresight
insight	ironclad	outrage	taskmaster	trailblazer

_____ 1. ability to predict and plan for the future

_____ 2. a boss demanding hard work

_____ 3. to shock and anger

_____ 4. firm; not changeable

_____ 5. a pioneer

_____ 6. understanding

_____ 7. to force someone to believe something

_____ 8. a large amount of unfinished work

_____ 9. sad

_____ 10. a drop; becoming worse

PART 1 EXERCISES

CONTEXT: ITEMS 1–9: Choose the best answer. **ITEM 10:** Circle true (T) or false (F).

a. backlog	b. brainwash	c. downcast	d. downturn	e. foresight
f. insight	g. ironclad	h. outrage	i. taskmaster	j. trailblazer

_____ 1. When this terrible and shameful scandal becomes known, it will cause public ___.

_____ 2. The two partners had a(n) ___ contract, and neither one could change the terms.

_____ 3. I became ___ when I realized that I would not graduate on time.

_____ 4. Overnight, there was a(n) ___ in the temperature, and it became very cold.

_____ 5. My boss was a(n) ___ who insisted that we do the job perfectly.

_____ 6. The physician was a(n) ___ who developed a new way of treating cancer.

_____ 7. We have a three-week ___ of orders that we must fill before we can take new ones.

_____ 8. The leader of the <u>bizarre</u> cult tried to ___ people into following his orders.

_____ 9. A course in psychology gave me ___ into how people think and behave.

T   F   10. If you have the *foresight* to plan ahead, you are less likely to have a *backlog* of assignments.

DERIVATIONS: Write the correct word form using the choices below.

1. That was a very _____ analysis of the novel. (**insight, insightful**)

2. It is _____ for an adult to throw such a temper tantrum. (**outrage, outrageous**)

3. He was _____ into believing what his kidnapper told him. (**brainwash, brainwashed**)

FINISH UP: Complete each sentence with a phrase of your choice.

4. I'm glad that I had the *foresight* to _____

_____.

5. Since you made an *ironclad* promise, _____

_____.

GIVE EXAMPLES: Answer the questions with your personal responses

6. Give an example of how a *downcast* person might behave.

7. Describe a <u>stringent</u> *taskmaster* you have known or heard about.

8. Identify one *trailblazer* and tell why you have identified this person.

9. Give one example of a *downturn* in business.

10. Give an example of what you might do if you had a *backlog* of work.

DESCRIPTIONS: Choose the word that these examples best describe.

_____ 1. seven assignments that are late; work piled up on your desk; fifty e-mails that need to be answered
       a. brainwash   **b.** taskmaster   **c.** foresight   **d.** backlog

_____ 2. how you feel when a pet dies; a <u>deterioration</u> in your happiness; how you feel when you can't afford to go out with friends;
       a. brainwash   **b.** trailblazer   **c.** downcast   **d.** backlog

_____ 3. being <u>thrifty</u> and saving money for college when you are in high school; buying lots of food now because prices will rise in the future; a couple buying a big house so they have room for future children
       a. foresight   **b.** downturn   **c.** backlog   **d.** ironclad

_____ 4. forced beliefs; only exposing children to one way of thinking; cult members making someone adopt their ideas
       a. ironclad   **b.** brainwash   **c.** outrage   **d.** foresight

_____ 5. great anger that is justified; what you feel when you are cheated; what you feel when you read about teenagers beating up an elderly woman
       a. outrage   **b.** trailblazer   **c.** backlog   **d.** downcast

STRATEGY PRACTICE: Using Context Clues of Substitution

To use context clues of substitution, think of a word (or phrase) that would substitute for an unknown word in a sentence. This is likely to be the definition of the unknown word. Practice this strategy by writing what you predict each word in italics means below.

1. As the plane *ascends*, the buildings on the ground appear to get smaller and smaller.

   Ascends means _____.

2. I am so *famished* that I could eat seven hamburgers.

   Famished means _____.

3. Their *expeditions* included a car trip across Canada.

   Expeditions means _____.

4. You will have to run at *breakneck* speed to win the race.

   Breakneck means _____.

5. The *aphorism* "lost time is never found again" is very true.

   Aphorism means _____.

PART 2: VALUABLE WORDS

acquire	affiliation	dominant	endeavor	entitlement
inevitable	obstinate	spouse	trauma	volatile

Use context clues to predict what some lesson words mean.

I will *endeavor* to help you, and I hope that I can. _____

Your boyfriend is not a *spouse* until you marry him. _____

11. acquire (ə-kwīr′) *verb*
   to get or buy something
   Unfortunately, some patients **acquire** infections at hospitals.
   After having a loan approved, he **acquired** the car.
   acquisition *noun*   The museum makes *acquisitions* of modern art.

12. affiliation (ə-fĭl′ē-ā′shən) *noun*
   a formal connection with an organization
   An **affiliation** with a union often improves pay for workers.
   Do you have a religious **affiliation?**
   affiliate (ə-fĭl′ē-āt) *verb*   Several small pharmacies *affiliated* into a network.
   affiliate (ə-fĭl′ē-ĭt) *noun*   The Anaheim Ducks and Buffalo Sabres are *affiliates* of the American Hockey League.

   > Note these differences in pronunciation:
   > affiliate (verb) ə-fĭl′ē-āt
   > affiliate (noun) ə-fĭl′ē-ĭt

13. dominant (dŏm′ə-nənt) *adjective*
   most powerful or strong
   The genes for brown eyes are **dominant** over those for blue eyes.
   Google is currently the **dominant** engine for computer searches.
   dominate *verb*   With 20 of 26 points, Ann *dominated* the scoring.

14. endeavor (ĕn-dĕv′ər)
   a. *verb* to try hard
   I **endeavored** to improve my vocabulary.
   b. *noun* an attempt that involves risk or difficulty
   Climbing a rock wall is an **endeavor** that requires courage.
   The professor's latest **endeavor** is a book on the history of jazz.

15. entitlement (ĕn-tīt′l-mənt) *noun*
   something you have a right to receive
   The right to vote is an **entitlement** of citizenship.
   Social Security payments are **entitlements** for U.S. senior citizens.
   entitle *verb*   Enrolling in the program *entitles* you to discounts.

endeavoring to reach the top

© R. Gino Santa Maria/shutterstock.com

16. inevitable (ĭn-ĕv′ĭ-tə-bəl) *adjective*
    certain to happen
    > It is **inevitable** that dead leaves will fall from trees.
    > If you do things too fast, mistakes are **inevitable**.
    inevitability *noun*   Death is an *inevitability* for all living things.

17. obstinate (ŏb′stə-nĭt) *adjective*
    stubborn; unwilling to change
    > Although his eyes were closing, the **obstinate** child refused to take a nap.
    > My **obstinate** grandmother refused to use a computer, no matter how much we showed how it could help her.
    obstinately *adverb*   He *obstinately* refused to change his opinion.

18. spouse (**spous**) *noun*
    a husband or wife; a marriage partner
    > The wives complained that their **spouses** did not do housework.
    spousal *adjective*   *Spousal* abuse is receiving public attention.

19. trauma (trô′-mə; trou′-mə) *noun*
    an injury or shocking negative event
    > The **trauma** from the fall caused permanent brain damage.
    > Victims of abuse may never recover from the **trauma.**
    traumatic *adjective*   Experiences of warfare can be *traumatic*.
    traumatize *adjective*   He was *traumatized* by the violent attack.

> A *trauma* is often a mental experience that causes long-term unhappiness or stress.

20. volatile (vŏl′ə-tl) *adjective*
    likely to change in an extreme or violent way; changing rapidly
    > The child's **volatile** moods swung from joy to anger.
    > United Nations troops kept order in the **volatile** region.
    volatility *noun*   A financial crisis caused *volatility* in stock prices.

DEFINITIONS: Write the correct word for each meaning.

acquire	affiliation	dominant	endeavor	entitlement
inevitable	obstinate	spouse	trauma	volatile

_____ 1. to get or buy

_____ 2. to try hard

_____ 3. most powerful

_____ 4. connection with an organization

_____ 5. marriage partner

_____ 6. stubborn

_____ 7. something you have a right to receive

_____ 8. injury; shocking negative event

_____ 9. changing rapidly

_____ 10. certain to happen

PART 2 EXERCISES

CONTEXT: ITEMS 1–9: Choose the best answer. **ITEM 10:** Circle true (T) or false (F).

a. acquire	b. affiliation	c. dominant	d. endeavor	e. entitlement
f. inevitable	g. obstinate	h. spouse	i. trauma	j. volatile

_____ 1. I speak English and Spanish, but English is my stronger and more ___ language.

_____ 2. The couple went into therapy to try to cope with the ___ of their child's death.

_____ 3. In this state, discounts at museums are a(n) ___ for senior citizens.

_____ 4. The ___ man refused to change his mind, despite evidence that he was wrong.

_____ 5. If you are married, you and your ___ usually file a joint tax return.

_____ 6. Starting your own business is a(n) ___ that requires lots hard work and some luck.

_____ 7. As Internet communication increases, I think it is ___ that the mail will be used less.

_____ 8. After being steady for years, the price of cotton has become ___ and changes rapidly.

_____ 9. The political candidate changed his ___ from the Democratic to the Republican party.

T   F   10. People should *endeavor* to *acquire* more debt.

DERIVATIONS: Write the correct word form using the choices below.

1. Because of his _____, the slightest thing could make him angry. **(volatile, volatility)**

2. The challenger _____ to defeat the champion. **(endeavor, endeavored)**

3. A wedding ring is a symbol of a _____ commitment. **(spousal, spouse)**

4. The hospital is an _____ of a well-known health system. **(affiliation, affiliate)**

5. Things never stay the same, so change is an _____. **(inevitable, inevitability)**

6. My boyfriend _____ refused to change the way he dressed. **(obstinate, obstinately)**

FINISH UP: Complete each sentence with a detailed phrase.

7. **Something I would love to *acquire* is** _____

_____.

8. **The *dominant* person in the conversation** _____

_____.

GIVE EXAMPLES: Answer the questions with your personal responses

9. Give an example of a *trauma* that would <u>alter</u> your life.

10. List a government *entitlement* available to children.

PASSAGE: The Lion Sleeps Tonight: A Story of Injustice

Fill in the word from each column's list that fits best.

Column Choices 1: affiliation, dominant, insight, taskmasters, trailblazer, traumatic

Column 2 Choices: acquire, dominant, endeavored, entitled, foresight, spouse

"In the jungle, the mighty jungle, the lion sleeps tonight" are the first words of a famous song. Do you remember the "eeeee"'s above the melody? The song topped charts in 36 countries, and it initiated a new musical style. But although he was a musical

(1)_____, the man who wrote it died in poverty.

The life of South African singer and composer

Solomon Linda gives us (2) _____ into the terrible conditions for black people there during much of the 1900s. The *outrageous* "apartheid," system they lived under was designed to keep whites

(3) _____ over blacks. Strictly enforced, *ironclad* laws forbade many blacks from living where they wanted. Black men who got jobs were allowed to move to cities, but apartheid laws often required that their *spouses* and children stay back in the countryside. This resulted in

(4) _____ separations of family members.

Laws also limited the rights of blacks to own property, get an education, and enter into contracts.

This discrimination against blacks allowed white

bosses to be harsh (5) _____.

Solomon Linda was a black Zulu migrant worker, with a gift for music. In 1939, he recorded "Mbube," meaning "The Lion," for Gallo records. The song came from Linda's childhood memories of guarding sheep from lion attacks.

The recording was a hit in South Africa, but apartheid laws made it *inevitable* that Linda would be cheated. The song sold over 100,000 copies, but he negotiated a payment of less than $2 for himself.

"The Lion," however, went on to greater fame. In the 1950s, it was sent to a company in the United States, and rescued from a pile of rejects by

Alan Lomax. He had the (6) _____ to realize that it might make money. Lomax brought it to folk singer Pete Seeger. Seeger changed the arrangement, named it "Wimoweh," and scored a hit. Seeger did not realize that he needed to

(7) _____ the rights to the song, but he did send some money to Linda.

Next, the Tokens, recorded the song, as "The Lion Sleeps Tonight" and it became an even bigger hit. The record company they were *affiliated* with copyrighted it in the name of a fictional person. This allowed two real people from the company to collect money.

Meanwhile, Linda died at the age of 53, not able to buy the drugs that would have saved his life. His

(8) _____ and daughters could not even afford a proper religious burial.

However, the family fortunes were about to change. In 2000, Rian Malan wrote an article about Linda that got worldwide attention. Malan estimated that other people had made over $15 million dollars from Linda's song. A lawsuit was initiated that

(9) _____ to get Linda's family more compensation. Lawyers claimed that he was

(10) _____ to a *backlog* of payments under a 1911 law. The resulting settlement gave Linda's family enough to live a comfortable life.

So the next time you hear those "eeeee"'s think of Solomon Linda, the creative genius who suffered under apartheid, but gave the world a haunting song.

Think About the Passage

1. How does Linda's life give *insight* into life for blacks under apartheid?

2. How did being recorded in the U.S. change what happened to the song?

ARGUMENT AND AGREEMENT; VALUABLE WORDS

PART 1: ARGUMENT AND AGREEMENT

coalition	controversial	domineering	endure	estranged
faction	proponent	relinquish	treacherous	wary

Argument and agreement are parts of our lives. Use context clues to predict the meanings of some words taught in this lesson.

We had to *endure* several hours of a boring lecture. _____

Sharks made the water *treacherous* for swimming._____

1. **coalition** (kō′ə-lĭsh′ən) *noun*
   a number of groups or people temporarily working together
   > A **coalition** of ten unions joined forces to promote workers' rights.
   > Six nations formed a **coalition** to combat illegal smuggling of weapons.

2. **controversial** (kŏn′trə-vûr′shəl) *adjective*
   causing disagreement, debate, or different opinions
   > Abortion is a **controversial** issue in the United States.
   > **controversy** *noun*   There is great *controversy* over the death penalty.

3. **domineering** (dŏm′ə-nîr′ĭng) *adjective*
   controlling of other people
   > His **domineering** mother chose his college and his major.

4. **endure** (ĕn-dōor′) *verb*
   a. to suffer difficulty for a long time
   > The hero **endured** torture without giving information to the enemy.
   > We had to **endure** a long, <u>tedious</u> wait to get the tickets.
   b. to last for a long time
   > The Hebrew language has **endured** for over five thousand years.
   > **endurance** *noun*   Exercise will increase your *endurance* for running.

5. **estranged** (ĭ-strānjd′) *adjective*
   separated because of negative feelings
   > The **estranged** women were best friends until one stole the other's husband.
   > The **estranged** couple did not even communicate about child care.
   > **estrangement** *noun*   An *estrangement* from one's family can lead to lonely holidays.

6. **faction** (făk′shən) *noun*
   a small disagreeing group within a larger group
   > A **faction** of dissatisfied members felt that the club president should resign.
   > Several **factions** battled for control of the city

Nations can form *coalitions*.

© AN BALCIOGLU/shutterstock.com

People who are *estranged* once had a close relationship, but have fought, and no longer communicate. If they are married, they no longer live together.

7. **proponent (prə-pō′nənt)** *noun*
   a public supporter
   > **Proponents** of recycling want special bins placed in every building.
   > The **proponent** of year-round schooling presented proof that summer vacation had negative <u>effects</u> on learning.

8. **relinquish (rĭ-lĭng′kwĭsh)** *verb*
   to give up something
   > The dictator was forced to **relinquish** power.
   > The dog <u>obstinately</u> refused to **relinquish** the bone.

9. **treacherous (trĕch′ər-əs)** *adjective*
   a. having hidden dangers
   > Enemy soldiers hiding near the road made her escape **treacherous.**
   b. not able to be trusted
   > Mandy's **treacherous** friend gossiped about her behind her back.
   treachery *noun*   People were shocked by *treachery* of the spy.

> *Treacherous* and *treachery* usually refer to secret, hidden, or unexpected harm.

10. **wary (wâr′ē)** *adjective*
    cautious; suspicious
    > We were **wary** of going home after the flood because more rain was <u>predicted</u>.
    > The store manager kept a **wary** eye on the teenager who he thought was shoplifting.
    wariness *noun*   He watched with *wariness* as the baby went down the stairs.

DEFINITIONS: Write the correct word for each meaning.

coalition	controversial	domineering	endure	estranged
faction	proponent	relinquish	treacherous	wary

_____ 1. supporter

_____ 2. to give up

_____ 3. groups of people temporarily working together

_____ 4. separated by negative feelings

_____ 5. cautious

_____ 6. a small, disagreeing group

_____ 7. to last a long time

_____ 8. causing disagreement or debate

_____ 9. controlling of other people

_____ 10. dangerous

PART 1 EXERCISES

CONTEXT: ITEMS 1–9: Choose the best answer. **ITEM 10:** Circle true (T) or false (F).

a. coalition	b. controversial	c. domineering	d. endure	e. estranged
f. faction	g. proponent	h. relinquish	i. treacherous	j. wary

_____ 1. There are many different opinions about ___ issues like gun control.

_____ 2. The ___ boss wouldn't let his employees make any decisions.

_____ 3. The five churches formed a(n) ___ to raise money for hungry children.

_____ 4. He found it hard to ___ his sister's constant screaming.

_____ 5. The man decided to ___ his seat, and give it to the pregnant woman.

_____ 6. Icy roads are ___, so be careful how you drive.

_____ 7. After their fight, the two friends became ___ and no longer spoke.

_____ 8. People should be ___ of giving out personal information to strangers.

_____ 9. The ___ of technology urged schools to buy every student a laptop.

T   F   10. A *faction* is usually a *proponent* of the majority view.

DERIVATIONS: Write the correct word form using the choices below.

1. The Roman empire _____ for over four hundred years. (**endure, endured**)

2. Zoo workers practice _____ when handling lions. (**wariness, wary**)

3. Double crossing your <u>ally</u> is an act of _____. (**treachery, treacherous**)

4. There is some _____ over changing the law. (**controversial, controversy**)

5. Many <u>thrifty</u> students are _____ of textbook rentals. (**proponents, proponent**)

6. The dictator _____ power a year ago. (**relinquished, relinquishing**)

FINISH UP: Complete each sentence with a detailed phrase.

7. **Since my uncle and I are *estranged*,** _____

_____.

8. **Seven political rights organizations formed a *coalition* to** _____

_____.

GIVE EXAMPLES: Answer with personal responses.

9. Give an example of something two *factions* would do.

10. Give two examples of what a *domineering* person might do.

DESCRIPTIONS: Choose the word that these examples best describe.

_____ 1. a hidden enemy waiting to attack; a person you think is a friend, but who <u>deviously</u> reveals your secrets; a harmless looking snake that is poisonous
    a. treacherous   **b.** domineering   **c.** estranged   **d.** wary

_____ 2. do not let anyone else talk; make all the decisions without asking anyone else; tell your husband what to do
    a. domineering   **b.** coalition   **c.** endure   **d.** proponent

_____ 3. a ten-year <u>negotiation</u>; suffering pain for months; a 100-year-old woman
    a. estranged   **b.** faction   **c.** controversial   **d.** endure

_____ 4. give up your house; resign from being leader; return jewelry to people who claim they own it
    a. wary   **b.** faction   **c.** relinquish   **d.** coalition

_____ 5. three civil rights groups working to pass a law against discrimination; ten countries banding together to provide emergency food relief; five government unions working to protect their pensions
    a. relinquish   **b.** estranged   **c.** coalition   **d.** endure

STRATEGY PRACTICE: Using Context Clues of Definition

A word can actually be defined for you in context. Practice this strategy by writing what you predict each word in italics means below.

1. My life has had many *vicissitudes*, and my best friend has had many changes too.

   Vicissitudes means _____.

2. The fisherman needed to buy hooks, reels, *gaffs*, and other types of equipment.

   Gaff means _____.

3. We explored the *Bet-pak Dala*, a desert in Kazakhstan.

   Bet-pak Dala means _____.

4. We were *fatigued*—which is to say, tired—after the walk.

   Fatigued means _____.

5. We drank soft drinks, and likewise *imbibed* lemonade and water.

   Imbibed means _____.

PART 2: VALUABLE WORDS

approximate	conventional	deficit	equate	fiscal
goad	hinder	peer	strife	verbatim

Some words in this section also deal with agreement and argument. Use context clues to predict what this lesson word means.

Disagreements *hindered* our efforts to make peace. _____

11. approximate
    a. *adjective* (ə-prŏk′sə-mĭt) about; not exact
       The **approximate** cooking time is two hours, but it may take more.
    b. *verb* (ə-prŏk′sə -māt′) to make a close estimate; to be similar
       We can **approximate** the shipping cost when you place the order for the clothes and then bill you the exact amount when we send them.
       This whistle can **approximate** many bird calls.
    approximately *adverb*   The room holds *approximately* 90 people.
    approximation *noun*   Can you give us an *approximation* of the time needed?

> Be careful! *Approximate* has two different meanings, two parts of speech, and two pronunciations!

12. conventional (kən-vĕn′shə-nəl) *adjective*
    a. usual; customary
       Since **conventional** medicine didn't help, she tried acupuncture.
       For some people, texting has replaced **conventional** phone calls.
    b. traditional; old-fashioned rather than new and imaginative
       The **conventional** man wore a suit and tie to the office every day.
       Inventors do not approach problems in **conventional** ways.
    convention *noun*   He follows the *convention* of opening doors for women.

> A *convention* can also be a conference.

13. deficit (dĕf′ĭ-sĭt) *noun*
    an amount that is lacking
       With a billion-dollar **deficit,** the state can no longer pay its bills.
       The team overcame a twelve-point **deficit** to win the game.

14. equate (ĭ-kwāt′) *verb*
    to make equal; to consider things to be equal
       Mom **equated** the portions, giving three potatoes to each child.
       We can't **equate** the crimes of armed robbery and shoplifting.

15. fiscal (fĭs′kəl) *adjective*
    relating to money, especially in government
       Several states must raise their taxes because of **fiscal** problems.
       At the end of its **fiscal** year, the company reported its profits.
    fiscally *adverb*   A government should be *fiscally* responsible.

16. goad (gōd) *verb*
    to cause people to react by annoying or angering them; to provoke
    > The bullies **goaded** the boy into fighting by teasing him.
    > My mom **goaded** me into cleaning my room by threatening not to let me have the car.

17. hinder (hĭnd'ər) *verb*
    to make something harder to do; to put at a disadvantage
    > Her fear of blood **hindered** her efforts to become a nurse.
    > Carrying heavy packages will **hinder** your ability to run.
    > **hindrance** *noun*   A lack of parking is a *hindrance* to shopping.

18. peer (pîr)

A *peer* is also a nobleman.

  a. *noun* a person who is equal to another in age, job, or position
    > The social worker observed the child playing with his **peers.**
    > After work, I spend time with my **peers,** but not with my boss.
  b. *verb* to look intently or carefully
    > He **peered** through the window, hoping to see something in the darkness.

19. strife (strīf) *noun*
    disagreement; fighting
    > **Strife** between the man and his wife led to a divorce.
    > A peace agreement ended the **strife** in the region.

strife

© Monkey Business Images/shutterstock.com

20. verbatim (vər-bā'tĭm) *adjective*
    using exactly the same words
    > Parrots can repeat **verbatim** the words that are taught to them.
    > A court reporter must type **verbatim** every word in a trial.

DEFINITIONS: Write the correct word for each meaning.

approximate	conventional	deficit	equate	fiscal
goad	hinder	peer	strife	verbatim

_____ 1. not exact

_____ 2. usual, customary

_____ 3. to make something harder to do

_____ 4. to make equal

_____ 5. using exactly the same words

_____ 6. disagreement; fighting

_____ 7. an amount that is lacking

_____ 8. to cause people to react

_____ 9. relating to money

_____ 10. to look carefully

PART 2 EXERCISES

CONTEXT: ITEMS 1–9: Choose the best answer. **ITEM 10:** Circle true (T) or false (F).

a. approximate	b. conventional	c. deficit	d. equate	e. fiscal
f. goad	g. hinder	h. peer	i. strife	j. verbatim

_____ 1. Since you left out a few words, you didn't repeat what I said ___.

_____ 2. The position of the sun in the sky gives a(n) ___ time, but a clock gives an exact time.

_____ 3. Two times two will ___ to four.

_____ 4. The child and her ___, who was in the same class, were best friends.

_____ 5. Since the city is spending more money than it takes in, it has a(n) ___.

_____ 6. It is ___ for people in the United States to shake hands when they meet.

_____ 7. Not taking your medicine will ___ your recovery.

_____ 8. Insulting the police may ___ them into arresting you.

_____ 9. I am tired of this ___; let's make up and be friends.

T F 10. A large *deficit* is a *fiscal* problem for a government.

DERIVATIONS: Write the correct word form using the choices below.

1. _____ through the binoculars, I saw many birds. (**Peer, Peering**)

2. I will attend a _____ in Denver. (**conventional, convention**)

3. We need _____ ten pounds of salad for the party. (**approximately, approximate**)

4. Borrowing money at high interest rates is not a good _____ policy. (**fiscally, fiscal**)

5. Because of your extravagance, there are _____ in two accounts. (**deficit, deficits**)

6. Laziness is a _____ to success. (**hindering, hindrance**)

FINISH UP: Complete each sentence with a detailed phrase.

7. I would *equate* the pain of having blood drawn from my arm with _____

_____.

8. One thing that should be repeated *verbatim* is _____

_____.

GIVE EXAMPLES: Answer with personal responses.

9. Give an example of *strife* that you have witnessed.

10. Give one way that you could *goad* someone into training harder for a race.

PASSAGE: TV: Good or Bad?

Fill in the word from each column's list that fits best.

Column 1 Choices: approximately, endured, fiscal, goad, peers, strife

Column 2 Choices: coalitions, domineering, equate, hindrance, proponents, verbatim

That screen we sit in front of at home has been a source of great *controversy*. The debate over whether TV is good or bad has

(1) _____ for more than fifty years.

One thing is clear: We watch a lot of TV. According to one source, parents talk with children for less than 60 minutes a week, but the average child

watches TV for (2) _____ 1700 minutes a week. Each year, a child spends about 900 hours in school, and 1500 in front of the TV.

Many studies *equate* watching too much TV with problems. Researchers found that people who were not satisfied with their lives spent 30% more time in front of a TV <u>monitor</u>.

TV is also associated with language *deficits*. When children watch TV in silence, parents are *relinquishing* opportunities to talk with them. But TV can even be *treacherous* if it is just playing in the background. Studies showed that families talk 15% less when the TV is on, even if no one is watching.

Violence on TV has <u>effects</u> on children. In the 1950s, a study found that those who watched violent cartoons were more likely to exhibit <u>volatile</u> behavior

and attack their (3) _____ . After television was introduced to three communities in

Canada, evidence of (4) _____, like black eyes and fist fights, increased. In 1994, a research team found that boys who were exposed to TV violence became *estranged* from normal human feelings of sympathy, and were more willing to

(5) _____ others into violent actions.

Children who watch more than four hours of television a day tend to be more overweight than their *peers*. Perhaps this is because those hours could be

spent playing sports or exercising. In this way, TV is

a(n) (6) _____ to physical fitness. In addition, one source estimates that in four hours of cartoons, there are 200 advertisements for junk food. Thousands of children can repeat these ads

(7) _____.

For all these reasons, many people have become

wary of TV. In fact, (8) _____ of community groups have sponsored National TV Turnoff Weeks.

But wait a second! Is TV all bad? Of course not!

Many (9) _____ of TV remind us that watching educational programs can increase achievement.

Some interesting data suggest that TV can even help change society. Studies done in rural India found that the introduction of TV affected life there. In this society, women do not traditionally have much power. Wives have often been taught to obey husbands and mothers-in-law, who may be very

(10) _____.

But, when TV was introduced, women suddenly saw a different type of society. Researchers believe that seeing examples of modern families on TV, even if it was in soap operas, gave these isolated women a sense of power. They became less tolerant of abuse, and girls began to get more schooling. In a short time, TV changed things that years of government reform efforts had not been able to <u>alter</u>.

So remember that TV can be good or bad. It can educate you, or just waste your time.

A man watching TV.

Think About the Passage

1. Give evidence from the passage that watching violent TV programs contributes to *strife*.

2. How did TV change *conventional* society in rural India?

FRIENDS AND FOES; VALUABLE WORDS

PART 1: FRIENDS AND FOES

acquaint	aloof	betray	clan	colleague
hospitable	intimate	protégé	rapport	timid

These words describe the friends and enemies that we all have. Use context clues to predict what some lesson words mean.

My *colleagues* and I go out to lunch near work. _____

You don't know each other, so let me *acquaint* you. _____

1. acquaint (ə-kwānt') *verb*
   a. to meet somebody; to introduce
      Let me **acquaint** you with my family.
   b. to give information about; to know about
      We would like to **acquaint** you with the facts.
      acquaintance *noun*   I have made several *acquaintances* in my class.

2. aloof (ə-lōōf') *adjective*
   unfriendly; keeping a distance
      People often seem **aloof**, when actually they are just shy.
      She stood **aloof** from the crowd, calmly observing our excitement.
   aloofness *noun*   One sign of not being interested in dating someone is
      aloofness

3. betray (bĭ-trā') *verb*
   a. to harm someone who has trusted you; to be disloyal
      The spy **betrayed** his country by giving secrets to the enemy.
   b. to show something that you wish to remain secret
      Your shaking hands **betray** your nervousness.
   betrayal *noun*   The personal assistant was accused of *betrayal* when she
      wrote a book about the movie star's controversial personal life.

4. clan (klăn) *noun*
   a large family; a large group of friends
      Our **clan** is so big that we have to rent a room for parties.
   clannish *adjective*   It is difficult to marry into that *clannish* family.

5. colleague (kŏl'ēg') *noun*
   a person you work with; a member of the same profession
      My **colleague** and I proposed a new sales plan to our boss.
      The physician e-mailed his **colleague** in New York, asking for advice
      about a patient.

An *acquaintance* is usually not a close friend.

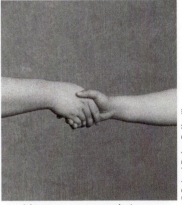

© Robert Erving Potter III

making an *acquaintance*

In Scotland, a *clan* meant a large group of related people, much like a tribe. Stories tell how *clans* fought and betrayed each other.

Two *colleagues* usually work at the same job level. You are NOT a *colleague* of your boss.

6. hospitable (hŏs′pĭ′-tə-bəl, hŏ-spĭt′ə-bəl) *adjective*
   a. welcoming to guests and visitors
      My **hospitable** roommate invited my friends to stay for dinner.
   b. providing good conditions for living things; welcoming
      Rocky mountain sides are not **hospitable** to trees.
      A lab that is <u>affiliated</u> with a university is a **hospitable** place for research.
   hospitality *noun*   Thank you for your *hospitality*!

> To be *intimate* can mean to have a sexual relationship.
>
> The verb *intimate* (ĭn′tə-māt′) means "to hint."

7. intimate (ĭn′tə-mĭt) *adjective*
   a. personal; private
      The **intimate** details of my dating life are not your business.
   b. having a very close relationship
      My best friend and I have been **intimate** since childhood.
   intimacy *noun*   The *intimacy* of the small club lent itself to romance.

8. protégé (prō′tə-zhā′) *noun*
   a person who is helped and guided by a more powerful person
      Rapper Lil Wayne helped to market the music of his **protégé**, Nicki
         Minaj.
      The congresswoman recommended her **protégé** for a job.

> *Protégé* and *rapport* come from French and have unusual pronunciations.
>
> *Protégé* can also appear as *protege*, without the accents.

9. rapport (ră-pôr′) *noun*
   understanding and trust
      The teacher's love of hip hop gave him instant **rapport** with students.
      College students from the same high school often develop **rapport**.

10. timid (tĭm′ĭd) *adjective*
    lacking self-confidence and courage; shy
       The **timid** student was nervous about the oral presentation he had to give.
    timidity *verb*   Her *timidity* made the job interview frightening.

DEFINITIONS: Write the correct word for each meaning.

acquaint	aloof	betray	clan	colleague
hospitable	intimate	protégé	rapport	timid

_____ 1. to harm someone who has trusted you

_____ 2. a person helped by a more powerful person

_____ 3. welcoming to guests

_____ 4. unfriendly

_____ 5. shy

_____ 6. understanding; trust

_____ 7. a person you work with

_____ 8. personal, private

_____ 9. a large family group

_____ 10. to introduce

PART 1 EXERCISES

CONTEXT: ITEMS 1–9: Choose the best answer. ITEM 10: Circle true (T) or false (F).

a. acquaint	b. aloof	c. betray	d. clan	e. colleague
f. hospitable	g. intimate	h. protégé	i. rapport	j. timid

_____ 1. Her ___ manner suggested that she did not want be friends with us.

_____ 2. The ___ boy was easily bullied, for he was afraid to fight back.

_____ 3. My ___ mother invited her sisters to stay at our house for a week.

_____ 4. Your boss should not know the ___ details of your personal life.

_____ 5. My ___ and I have equal experience and work responsibilities.

_____ 6. The corporation president trained his ___ for a leadership position.

_____ 7. You often find it easy to develop a(n) ___ with a person who shares your interests.

_____ 8. Our ___ of fifty people gathered for reunions each year.

_____ 9. I will never ___ my friend, and she knows she can trust me.

T   F   10. If you *acquaint* two people they will know the *intimate* details of each other's lives.

DERIVATIONS: Write the correct word form using the choices below.

1. Let me <u>convey</u> how it is nice to make your _____. (**acquaintance, acquaint**)

2. The _____ of your questions makes me uncomfortable. (**intimacy, intimate**)

3. As the others were busily gossiping, she maintained a position of _____. (**aloof, aloofness**)

4. I will never forgive your <u>devious</u> _____. (**betray, betrayal**)

5. They are _____ and don't socialize with outsiders. (**clan, clannish**)

6. Because of her _____, she was not a good saleswoman. (**timid, timidity**)

FINISH UP: Complete each sentence with a detailed phrase.

7. **The CEO thought that her *protégé*** _____

_____.

8. **A good *colleague*** _____

_____.

GIVE EXAMPLES: Answer with personal responses.

9. Give two examples of *hospitality*.

10. Give an example of someone with whom you have *rapport*, and explain why.

DESCRIPTIONS: Choose the word that these examples best describe.

_____ 1. afraid of people; not wanting to draw attention to yourself; fearful to participate in sports
   a. betray   **b.** timid   **c.** aloof   **d.** intimate

_____ 2. feeling that a person you have just met will become a close friend; having the same interests as another person; laughing over memories with your cousin
   a. colleague   **b.** clan   **c.** acquaint   **d.** rapport

_____ 3. not interested being friendly; refusing to join in a conversation; not talking to <u>colleagues</u>
   a. aloof   **b.** betray   **c.** rapport   **d.** protégé

_____ 4. two <u>affiliated</u> dentists; all the salespeople at work; people who work in the same department
   a. betray   **b.** acquaint   **c.** hospitable   **d.** colleague

_____ 5. sixteen sisters and their families; fifteen <u>peers</u> who are close friends; group of Scottish relatives
   a. clan   **b.** colleague   **c.** intimate   **d.** aloof

STRATEGY PRACTICE: Using Context Clues of Opposition

A context clue can signal an opposite meaning through the use of words like *not*, *but*, or *in contrast*. Practice this strategy by writing what you predict each word in italics means below.

1. No *neophytes* allowed; only experienced surfers can compete in this event.

   Neophytes means _____.

2. She never raises her voice, but her husband constantly *bellows*.

   Bellows means _____.

3. I asked her if we could go on an *excursion*, and she said "No, I want to stay at home."

   Excursion means _____.

4. He never walks fast, but only *saunters*.

   Saunters means _____.

5. I am usually in a good mood, and rarely feel *morose*.

   Morose means _____.

PART 2: VALUABLE WORDS

ancestor	companion	designate	leisure	maneuver
patron	sociable	solitary	vague	valid

Some of these words also deal with people and their feelings. Use context clues to predict what some lesson words mean.

He prefers to be *solitary* and not spend time with other people. _____

I spend my *leisure* time playing online games. _____

11. ancestor (ăn′sĕs′tər) *noun*
    a person you are descended from, especially one who lived in the past
    > DNA evidence suggests that ruler Genghis Khan, who lived 900 years ago, is the **ancestor** of about one in every 200 men.
    > My **ancestor** fought in the American Revolutionary War.
    ancestral (ăn-sĕs′trəl) *adjective*   The princess visited her **ancestral** castle.

12. companion (kəm-păn′yən) *noun*
    a. a person who keeps you company
    > My friend and I were **companions** on the trip.
    b. one part of a pair or group
    > This photo is a good **companion** to the one already on the wall.
    companionship *noun*   My dog gives me great *companionship*.

designating someone

© Robert Erving Potter III

13. designate (dēz′ĭg-nāt′) *verb*
    to choose for a purpose
    > The teacher **designated** one student as class leader.
    > This part of the shoreline has been **designated** as a nature preserve, and no buildings are allowed.
    designation *noun*   A landmark *designation* hung on the house.

14. leisure (lē′zhər)
    a. *noun* free time
    > Now that I am retired, I have more **leisure**.
    b. *adjective* referring to free time
    > Basketball is my favorite **leisure** activity.

> The phrase *at your (my, their) leisure* is common, as in "Please return my call *at your leisure.*" Here *leisure* means "when you can."

15. maneuver (mə-nōō′vər)
    a. *verb* to use skill to achieve something; to manipulate
    > By calming the wild horse, she **maneuvered** it into the barn.
    > The party leader **maneuvered** senators into voting for the bill by agreeing to compensate them with special favors.
    b. *noun* a complicated action
    > The lawyer tried a sophisticated **maneuver** to win the trial.
    > The general presented several new battle **maneuvers**.

> Often *maneuver* has the meaning of using dishonesty or cleverness.

16. patron (pā′trən) *noun*
   a. a regular customer
      I am a **patron** of our local café, where I go each morning.
   b. a person who supports artists or charities
      The pianist's **patron** sponsored a concert for him.
      The CEO is a **patron** of charities that support civil rights.
   patronize *verb* We like to *patronize* local businesses.

> To *patronize* can also mean to act superior or to be a snob.

17. solitary (sŏl′ĭ-tĕr′ē) *adjective*
   alone; being the only one
      As winter began, only a **solitary** leaf remained on the tree.
      He leads a **solitary** life, without friends, family, or social activities.

18. sociable (sō′shə-bəl) *adjective*
   friendly; liking to be with people
      Sociable people usually love to attend parties.
   sociability *noun* Because of her *sociability*, she enjoyed serving on committees.

19. vague (vāg) *adjective*
   not clear; not well defined
      His **vague** directions were, "Turn right in approximately three blocks, go for a mile or so, and look for a home near the corner."
   vaguely *adverb* I feel *vaguely* uncomfortable, though I don't know why.
   vagueness *noun* Because of *vagueness*, the students couldn't understand the exam question.

> Things are *vague* when people don't give enough details. If you ask for a meeting time, a *vague* answer would be "sometime this week."

20. valid (văl′ĭd) *adjective*
   a. legal and officially accepted
      Your passport is **valid** for ten years.
   b. based on strong facts or reasons
      I have **valid** concerns about my mother's health.
   validity *verb* Your facts are wrong, so your report lacks *validity*.

DEFINITIONS: Write the correct word for each meaning.

ancestor	companion	designate	leisure	maneuver
patron	sociable	solitary	vague	valid

_____ 1. a complicated action

_____ 2. alone

_____ 3. to choose for a purpose

_____ 4. regular customer

_____ 5. friendly; enjoying the company of others

_____ 6. free time

_____ 7. legal; officially accepted

_____ 8. person you are descended from

_____ 9. person who keeps you company

_____ 10. not clear

PART 2 EXERCISES

CONTEXT: ITEMS 1–9: Choose the best answer. **ITEM 10:** Circle true (T) or false (F).

a. ancestor	b. companion	c. designate	d. leisure	e. maneuver
f. patron	g. sociable	h. solitary	i. vague	j. valid

_____ 1. We would like to thank the ___ who gave the museum money for the exhibit.

_____ 2. If the police see that your driver's license is not ___, they will give you a ticket.

_____ 3. I can give you a(n) ___ definition of that word, but not an exact one.

_____ 4. The sergeant will ___ three soldiers to go on the mission.

_____ 5. If you are ___, you are likely to have lots of friends.

_____ 6. Reading is a(n) ___ way to spend time because it doesn't involve other people.

_____ 7. Don't hurry; you can finish this at your ___.

_____ 8. My ___ lived from 1708 to 1777.

_____ 9. She tried to ___ her husband into washing the dishes by saying she had a headache.

T F 10. If you have a *companion*, your trip is *solitary*.

DERIVATIONS: Write the correct word form using the choices below.

1. I am tired of your _____. Let's stay home tonight! **(sociable, sociability)**

2. How dare you _____ me by treating me like I am stupid! **(patron, patronize)**

3. The contract is not _____ because it is not signed. **(validity, valid)**

4. I am happy you will be my dinner _____. **(companionship, companion)**

5. My _____ was a farmer in Thailand. **(ancestor, ancestry)**

6. Your _____ answer suggests you are lying. **(vague, vaguely)**

FINISH UP: Complete each sentence with a detailed phrase.

7. **When I have some *leisure* time,** _____

_____.

8. **When I tried to *maneuver* the three suitcases into the tiny car trunk,** _____

_____.

GIVE EXAMPLES: Answer with personal responses.

9. Give three examples of *solitary* activities.

10. Whom in your family would you *designate* as a peacemaker? Why?

PASSAGE: Spa Treatments for Two-Year-Olds?

Fill in the word from each column's list that fits best.

Column 1 Choices: acquainted, designated, intimate, maneuver, patrons, vague

Column 2 Choices: colleagues, hospitable, leisure, rapport, timid, valid

At her first spa visit, a four-year-old becomes

(1) _____ with the process of getting her nails done and learns the word "exfoliate" when she gets her Strawberry Ice Cream Manicure. The mother of a two-year-old tries to

(2) _____ the baby into holding still while tanning lather is applied to the child's skin. Another mother's face *betrays* anxiety as she watches her eight-year-old daughter get her eyebrows tweezed. The mother finally shouts "No! Not like that!"

Over 5,500 years ago, one of our *ancestors* discovered that dark kohl could be used as eye makeup. Since then, women have been using beauty treatments. However, some of today's spa

(3) _____ are not even in elementary school. Their mothers treat these little girls as *protégés* who must be taught the art of being beautiful.

Working with a small child sometimes makes a spa worker *vaguely* uncomfortable, especially when it

involves (4) _____ areas of the body. After completing the eyebrows of the eight-

year-old, her mom wanted her to have a bikini wax. A spa worker was shocked, but tried to remain *aloof*, as the child was <u>escorted</u> to the next room, where a *colleague* had been (5)

_____ to deliver the service.

Spa services are now common for many teenagers. The mother of a fifteen-year-old reports

that the girl's school (6) _____ regularly get eyebrow waxing, manicures, and hair color.

All of this may strike some people as <u>outrageous</u>. Many mothers, however, say that, when they get spa services with daughters, they develop

(7) _____ with them. They find that the spa experience gives parent and child time to *socialize*.

But, in fact, these mothers may be teaching their daughters dangerous lessons. Spa treatments can help to convince children that appearance defines who you are, and so it is extremely important.

Popular culture often reinforces this. We constantly see images of physically perfect celebrities. Sadly, young people may try to imitate their looks and feel unhappy if they can't succeed. Mental health professionals say that this is unhealthy, and

they have (8) _____ concerns that are supported by research. Forty-two percent of girls from 6 to 8 years old want to lose weight. Cosmetic surgery has doubled in people 18 years and younger. Such insecurity has led to psychological problems.

Meanwhile, though, the personal services industry is profiting from new customers. Spas have become more and more

(9) _____ to young children.
Twenty years ago, these girls would have spent

their (10) _____ time riding bikes and building forts. Now they are getting facials.

Think About the Passage

1. According to the passage, what is one disadvantage of having children *patronize* spas?

2. According to the passage, how does popular culture try to *maneuver* the self-esteem of children?

This section will help you review words from Lessons 4, 5, and 6. It will also provide practice in the strategy of using context clues.

DEFINITIONS: Fill in the letter that matches the definition of each word. Use each choice only once.

_____	1. volatile	a.	unchangeable
_____	2. valid	b.	legal; officially accepted
_____	3. strife	c.	separated because of negative feelings
_____	4. inevitable	d.	fighting, disagreement
_____	5. designate	e.	a drop
_____	6. fiscal	f.	stubborn
_____	7. betray	g.	to choose for a purpose
_____	8. ironclad	h.	likely to change in an extreme way
_____	9. clan	i.	to be disloyal
_____	10. estranged	j.	a large family
		k.	certain to happen
		l.	relating to money

DERIVATIONS: Write the correct word form using the choices below.

1. The local union is an _____ of a national organization. (**affiliate, affiliation**)

2. Horror movies can _____ a child. (**traumatized, traumatize**)

3. Waving hands to say hello is a _____ in many parts of the world. (**conventional, convention**)

4. There is _____ over the new rules. (**controversial, controversy**)

5. Can you give me an _____ of the amount? (**approximate, approximation**)

6. Will this ruin the _____ of our friendship? (**intimately, intimacy**)

7. Laziness is a _____ to success. (**hinder, hindrance**)

57

CONTEXT: Write in the letter of the word that best completes each sentence. Use each choice only once.

a. aloof	b. deficit	c. domineering	d. downcast
e. faction	f. foresight	g. leisure	h. proponent
i. rapport	j. trailblazer	k. vague	l. volatile

_____ 1. Food prices were _____, and they quickly rose and fell.

_____ 2. Since she had two jobs and was a single parent, she didn't have much _____ time.

_____ 3. The physician was a(n) _____ who developed a new type of heart surgery.

_____ 4. He was _____ for several months after his close friend died.

_____ 5. If you write a $100 check, but only have $90 in the bank, you have a(n) _____.

_____ 6. Because of our excellent _____, we became close friends who often spent time together.

_____ 7. Since one _____ was usually fighting another for control of the club, there was constant arguing.

_____ 8. I don't trust her, and prefer not to be her friend, but to remain _____.

_____ 9. Twenty years ago, the businessman had the _____ to realize that online purchasing would become important.

_____ 10. I am a(n) _____ of children's rights and have made speeches on the topic.

PASSAGE: Real or Unreal?

Fill in the word from each column's list that fits best.

Column 1 Choices: acquainted, backlog, endeavored, insight, ironclad, maneuvers, outraged, treacherous

Column 2 Choices: acquire, endures, equate, goad, patrons, relinquished, solitary, timid

Many of us are (1) _____ with the names Johnny Appleseed, Robin Hood, Betty Crocker, and John Henry. But were these actual people?

The famous character Robin Hood supposedly fought against (2) the

_____

English King John, who stole the throne from his brother, King Richard. Robin's many clever

(3) _____ and tricks often made King John look foolish. According to legend, Robin robbed from the rich and gave to the poor. Of course,

Did Robin Hood exist?

this (4) _____ wealthy nobles.

Many scholars have (5) _____ to figure out if Robin was a real man. Perhaps he was, but because he lived more than 900 years ago, it is

impossible to get (6) _____ proof of his existence.

Aunt Jemima, who is seen on many boxes of pancake mix, was a real person. In fact, she was two real people! The story goes that, after watching a demonstration, the owner of a flour company had the

(7) _____ to realize that if people actually saw a person making pancakes, they would buy more flour.

Aunt Jemima was first represented by African American Nancy Green. After she

(8) _____ the role, it was played by Anna Robinson. Although it has been many years since the Aunt Jemima figure has given demonstrations, her image

(9) _____ on boxes of pancake mix to this day.

Although General Mills published Betty Crocker's pictures and recipes for years, the lady

never existed. Still, (10) _____ who bought General Mills products loved the cheery face on packages. After 20 years of using her name, the company hired an actress to play her in 1949.

Johnny Appleseed was the nickname of a person named John Chapman. He was a(n)

(11) _____ figure, who roamed the American frontier alone, planting apple trees. Chapman lived from 1784 to 1845. His efforts greatly

helped farmers to (12) _____ the seeds for apple orchards.

Many people (13) _____ the names John Henry and Paul Bunyan with great strength. According to a famous story, John Henry, an African-American railroad worker, challenged a steam drill in a contest hammering railroad ties into the ground. His great *endurance* helped him to win, but, at the end of the contest, he collapsed and died. Paul Bunyan was a logger, who often did the impossible. Once he tried to

(14) _____ the weather into making a rain storm by getting it angry. Both figures are simply legends.

STRATEGY REVIEW: Use context clues to determine the meaning of each word in italics.

1. Children gather by the fireplace to listen to the stories that the sailor *recounts*.

   Recounts means _____.

2. We won't allow *diazidoethan* on the train because it is an explosive chemical.

   Diazidoethan means _____.

3. The school does not provide uniforms *gratis,* so you must pay for them.

   Gratis means _____.

4. The food at the picnic was so *copious* that we had many leftovers.

   Copious means _____.

5. The *egregious* calculation error was so serious that it made the whole experiment fail.

   Egregious means _____.

6. No imitations are allowed, so don't try to *emulate* someone else.

   Emulate means _____.

7. We *dispatched* the package by express mail so it would get there in time for the holidays.

   Dispatched means _____.

8. The children *exasperated* their mother, and she became so annoyed that she lost her temper.

   Exasperated means _____.

9. A happy ending was revealed at the *denouement* of the play.

   Denouement means _____.

10. The child was *deluded* into thinking that the streets of the U.S. were made of gold.

    Deluded means _____.

STRATEGY: THE DICTIONARY AND CONTEXT

INTRODUCTION

As you study, you will need strategies for figuring out the meaning of unknown words. So far, this book has presented two of these: using the dictionary (Section 1) and using context clues (Section 2). In Section 3, you will practice these skills in combination.

THE DICTIONARY

This dictionary entry for *employ* has some advanced features.

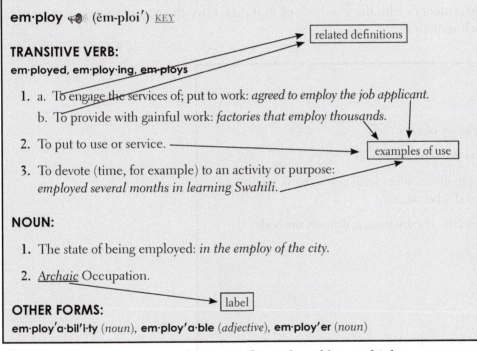

This complex word serves as a few parts of speech and has multiple meanings. It also has three related words listed. Actually, there is at least one more: *Employment* gets its own entry in the dictionary.

   The entry also has a special-use label. The word *archaic* (in NOUN, definition 2) means that this definition of the word is no longer used. The abbreviation *obs.* (*obsolete*) also means this. Definitions that are labeled *nonstandard*, *informal*, or *slang* are not used in formal speech and writing. Labels like *law* or *chem.* (chemistry) indicate that a word has a special meaning in these fields.

   Phrases like *agreed to employ the job applicant* show examples of how to use the word.

   Finally, transitive verb, 1 has parts *a* and *b*, which are closely related definitions.

Houghton Mifflin Harcourt, *The American Heritage Dictionary of the English Language*, 4th ed., © 2009. Reprinted by permission.

Using the information in the definition, answer these questions:

1. Which definition is no longer used in English? _____

2. List the example of use for the noun 1 definition. _____

CONTEXT CLUES

Remember that context clues, are hints about word meaning in a sentence. Three types are:

Context clues of **substitution.** You can substitute a known word for an unknown word:
- She was *mortified* when she spilled sauce on her father-in-law. (*Mortified* means "embarrassed.")

Context clues of **definition.** The word is defined for you:
- It is *atrial fibrillation*, an abnormal heart rhythm. (*Atrial fibrillation* is "abnormal heart rhythm.")

Context clues of **opposition.** The opposite sense of a word is given.
- The boring speech was short, but it seemed *interminable*. (*Interminable* means long, endless.)

USING THE DICTIONARY AND CONTEXT CLUES

This dictionary entry is followed by sentences with the words *shock* in italics. Give the part of speech and definition number that best fits each sentence.

---

shock 🔊 (shŏk) <u>KEY</u>

NOUN:

1. A violent collision or impact; a heavy blow.

2. A severe offense to one's sense of decency; an outrage.

3. A potentially fatal body reaction to illness, injury, and dehydration; problems getting blood flow to the heart and other organs.

4. A muscle spasm caused by an electric current passing through the body.

5. A shock absorber.

VERB:

shocked, shock·ing, shocks

1. To surprise, disgust, or offend.

2. To give an animal or person an electric shock.

_____ 1. She received a *shock* when she touched the electric wire.

_____ 2. The patient may go into *shock* as a result of injury.

_____ 3. I needed new *shocks* on my car.

_____ 4. The violence in the movie will *shock* sensitive people.

_____ 5. The *shock* from the crash crushed my sister's leg.

WORDS TO GUIDE COLLEGE LEARNING; VALUABLE WORDS

PART 1: WORDS TO GUIDE COLLEGE LEARNING

assess	assumption	cite	implication	inquisitive
integrate	precision	rational	rigorous	terminology

This list focuses on words commonly used in college courses. You need them to do assignments, perform experiments, and take tests. Use context clues to predict what these lesson words mean.

The coach *assessed* Luke's skill by watching him play. _____

Can you *integrate* these two paragraphs into one? _____

1. assess (ə-sĕs′) *verb*
   a. to judge; to evaluate
   The business used a checklist to **assess** customer satisfaction.
   The pawn broker **assessed** the value of my watch at $100.
   b. to charge a tax or a fine
   I was **assessed** $60 for damaging city property.
   assessment *noun*   The store asked for an *assessment* of customer service.

assessing customer satisfaction

2. assumption (ə-sŭmp′shən) *noun*
   something unproven that is accepted as true
   Your economic forecast makes many **assumptions** about job growth.
   Never make the **assumption** that teenagers will obey school rules.
   assume *verb*   He *assumed* it would be warm, so he didn't bring a coat.

3. cite (sīt) *verb*
   to use as an expert opinion or example; to quote
   I **cited** two books to support the points in my paper.
   The speaker **cited** Al Gore on the dangers of global warming.
   citation *noun*   The footnote gave the source of my *citation*.

> A *citation* can also be a call to appear in a court of law. Or it can be praise for good behavior: *He was cited for bravery.*

4. implication (ĭm′plĭ-kā′shən) *noun*
   a hint; something not stated directly
   When mom replied "Let's wait and see" to my request for a loan, the **implication** was clearly "no."
   imply *verb*   Crying usually *implies* unhappiness.

5. inquisitive (ĭn-kwĭz′ĭ-tĭv) *adjective*
   questioning; eager for knowledge
   The **inquisitive** child wanted to know all about my personal life.

> At times, *inquisitive* people may be *too* curious.

63

Integration also refers to combining minorities with the majority. After U.S. schools were *integrated* in the 1960s, all students, including African Americans, attended together.

6. **integrate** (ĭn′tĭ-grāt′) *verb*
   to combine; to join together into a larger whole
   > It can be difficult for immigrants to **integrate** into U.S. society.
   > Please **integrate** the ideas we talked about into your paper.
   integration *noun*   The *integration* of two software systems can be difficult.

7. **precision** (prĭ-sĭzh′ən) *noun*
   great accuracy; being very exact
   > Special tools enabled the craftsman to measure the opening with **precision**.
   precise *adjective*   I recall the *precise* moment I fell in love with you.
   precisely *adverb*   It is *precisely* two o'clock.

Don't confuse *rational* with *rationale*. A *rationale* refers to the reasons for something.

8. **rational** (răsh′ə-nəl) *adjective*
   based on reason; logical; not based on emotion
   > His **rational** speech explains <u>precisely</u> the reasons for raising taxes.
   > I know it is not **rational** to be afraid of the dark, but I am.
   rationality *noun*   Four-year-olds often don't understand appeals to *rationality*.
   rationally *adverb*   Let's approach this problem *rationally*.

9. **rigorous** (rĭg′ər-əs) *adjective*
   strict; difficult; harsh
   > Medical school has **rigorous** entrance requirements.
   > The university's **rigorous** standards for protecting students ensure that any research studies they participate in will not harm them.
   rigor *noun*   The *rigor* of the exercise program exhausted the track team.

10. **terminology** (tûr′mə-nŏl′ə-jē) *noun*   **plural: terminologies**
    the special vocabulary of a science, business, or profession
    > *Pyoderma* and *percutaneous* are examples of medical **terminology**.
    term *noun*   *Cyclonic* is a *term* used by people who specialize in studying weather. (A *term* is one word in a *terminology*.)

DEFINITIONS: Write the correct word for each meaning.

| assess | assumption | cite | implication | inquisitive |
| integrate | precision | rational | rigorous | terminology |

_____ 1. to combine

_____ 2. curious

_____ 3. special vocabulary

_____ 4. strict; difficult

_____ 5. logical

_____ 6. to judge; to evaluate

_____ 7. a hint

_____ 8. to quote

_____ 9. something unproven that is accepted as true

_____ 10. great accuracy

PART 1 EXERCISES

CONTEXT: ITEMS 1–9: Choose the best answer. **ITEM 10:** Circle true (T) or false (F).

| a. assess | b. assumption | c. cite | d. implication | e. inquisitive |
| f. integrate | g. precision | h. rational | i. rigorous | j. terminology |

_____ 1. Modern tests are very accurate and measure cholesterol level with ___.

_____ 2. The words *accumeter* and *subcooler* are part of air conditioning ___.

_____ 3. When people smile, the ___ is that they are happy.

_____ 4. Basic army training is ___, and it requires physical fitness, energy, and discipline.

_____ 5. The course will ___ reading and writing instruction so students can combine them better.

_____ 6. The ___ man annoyed me by constantly asking questions about my family.

_____ 7. This test will ___ your skills in mathematics, so we can see what you know.

_____ 8. If you don't believe me, I can ___ research that proves my point.

_____ 9. You can't make the ___ that you will pass the test without studying.

T   F   10. It is *rational* to base your conclusions on lots of *assumptions* and faulty reasoning.

DERIVATIONS: Write the correct word form using the choices below.

1. The _____ of the two sales forces went smoothly. (**integrate, integration**)

2. Running is _____ exercise. (**rigorous, rigor**)

3. Are you _____ that I am telling a lie? (**implied, implying**)

4. I _____ that you and your companion will go to the dance. (**assumption, assume**)

5. Please list your _____ at the end of the paper. (**cited, citations**)

FINISH UP: Complete each sentence with a detailed phrase.

6. **If I wanted to *assess* a car I was considering buying,** _____

_____.

7. **The *inquisitive* person** _____

_____.

8. **It is important to be *rational* when** _____

_____.

GIVE EXAMPLES: Answer with personal responses.

9. Choose a field that has its own *terminology* and list two *terms* from it.

10. Give an example of an activity that requires *precision* and explain why.

DESCRIPTIONS: Choose the word that these examples best describe.

_____ 1. pouring two liquids together; five new members joining a team; combining two companies
  a. cite   **b.** implication   **c.** rational   **d.** integrate

_____ 2. a <u>stringent</u> training program; lots of class requirements; a tightly constructed argument
  a. rigorous   **b.** assess   **c.** assumption   **d.** cite

_____ 3. making tiny measurements; being exactly on time; choosing your words very carefully
  a. implication   **b.** precision   **c.** terminology   **d.** integrate

_____ 4. a final exam; taking a sick person's temperature; the taxes you pay on a house
  a. rational   **b.** rigorous   **c.** implication   **d.** assess

_____ 5. asking lots of questions; constantly looking words up in the dictionary; requesting explanations for everything
  a. terminology   **b.** inquisitive   **c.** assess   **d.** integrate

STRATEGY PRACTICE: Combining Context Clues with the Dictionary

The entries that you find in a dictionary are often complex. Here is a dictionary entry for a word on your list. Read it and then give the part of speech and definition number that best fits each sentence.

> **cite** 🔊 (sīt) <u>KEY</u>
>
> **TRANSITIVE VERB:**
> **cit·ed, cit·ing, cites**
>
> 1. To quote as an authority or example.
>
> 2. To mention or bring forward as support, illustration, or proof: *cited several instances of insubordinate behavior.*
>
> 3. To honor formally.
>
> 4. To summon before a court of law.

_____ 1. He was *cited* and had to appear in court on April 15.

_____ 2. What he *cited* in the paper was "According to Einstein, time is variable."

_____ 3. In the ceremony, several firefighters were *cited* for their heroism, and they received awards.

_____ 4. Dorothy *cited* the many times that her sister had borrowed her car.

PART 2: VALUABLE WORDS

competent	escalate	exotic	habitually	impartial
reiterate	simultaneous	urgent	vulnerable	waive

You will find these words useful in a variety of ways. Use context clues to predict what one lesson word means.

Fees are *waived* for members, so they enter free _____.

11. competent (kŏmp′ĭ-tənt) *adjective*
    satisfactory; capable of doing a satisfactory job
    > I am **competent** to change a tire, but not to fix an engine.
    > We want to make sure that our physician is **competent**.
    competence *noun*   Practice helps to develop *competence*.

    > Sometimes *competent* means satisfactory, but NOT excellent.

12. escalate (ĕs′kə-lāt′) *verb*
    to increase in intensity or force
    > The disagreement **escalated** into a million-dollar law suit.
    > The unfriendly talk **escalated** into a shouting match.
    escalation *noun*   There has been an *escalation* in the rate of obesity.

    > Escalate is often used when bad things become worse, as in "The fighting escalated."

13. exotic (ĭg-zŏt′ĭk) *adjective*
    strange and unusual
    > Their **exotic** honeymoon was spent on the island of Bali.
    > The **exotic** strawberry poison frog, found in Central America, is vivid red and less than an inch long.

    > Exotic things are usually from far-away places.

14. habitually (hə-bĭch′ōō-əl-ē) *adverb*
    done usually or regularly
    > I **habitually** read, drink coffee, and check Facebook in the morning.
    > I am not surprised we are waiting, for he is **habitually** late.
    habit *noun*   I am in the *habit* of rising early.
    habitual *adjective*   Unfortunately, he was a *habitual* liar.

15. impartial (ĭm-pär′shəl) *adjective*
    fair; not favoring one side or the other
    > A judge is supposed to be **impartial**.
    > If you pick a favorite, you are not **impartial**.
    impartiality *noun*   Football fans questioned the referee's *impartiality* when he called an unfair foul on the visiting team.
    impartially *adverb*   Using a rubric, she evaluated essays *impartially*.

16. reiterate (rē-ĭt′ə-rāt′) *verb*
    to say or do again
    > I **reiterated** the directions to make sure he understood them.
    reiteration *noun*   The new policy statement was simply a *reiteration* of the old one.

simultaneous exercise movements

© Robert Erving Potter III

17. simultaneous (sī′məl-tā′nē-əs) *adjective*
    happening at the same time

   > **Simultaneous** broadcasts of the United Nations meeting were made in the United States, Berlin, and Cairo.

   > Public officials became alarmed when there were **simultaneous** outbreaks of *E. coli* poisoning in seven cities.

   simultaneously *adverb*   Two alarm clocks rang *simultaneously*.

18. urgent (ûr′jənt) *adjective*
    needing immediate attention

   > The professor left the class when she received an **urgent** message.

   > The **urgent** tone in the child's voice told us that we needed to take him to the bathroom right away.

   urgency *noun*   Because of the *urgency* of the situation, the police called the mayor at 2 AM.   **plural: urgencies**

19. vulnerable (vŭl′nər-ə-bəl) *adjective*
    easy to attack or hurt

   > The starving, poorly equipped army was **vulnerable** to enemy raids.

   > Using company money for extravagant personal expenses makes an employee **vulnerable** to being fired.

   vulnerability *noun*   Sensing his *vulnerability*, the bullies attacked the boy.

> Don't confuse *waive* with *wave*. The two words are pronounced the same. *Wave* means to move back and forth.

20. waive (wāv) *verb*
    to give up a right; not to require; not to enforce a rule

   > Because Lan was a published author, the college **waived** English 101 for her.

   > I foolishly **waived** my right to appoint a lawyer.

DEFINITIONS: Write the correct word for each meaning.

competent	escalate	exotic	habitually	impartial
reiterate	simultaneous	urgent	vulnerable	waive

_____ 1. to say again

_____ 2. easy to hurt

_____ 3. capable of doing a satisfactory job

_____ 4. to increase in force

_____ 5. not to enforce a rule

_____ 6. fair; not showing favor

_____ 7. needing immediate attention

_____ 8. happening at the same time

_____ 9. strange, unusual

_____ 10. done often and regularly

PART 2 EXERCISES

CONTEXT: ITEMS 1–9: Choose the best answer. **ITEM 10:** Circle true (T) or false (F).

a. competent	b. escalate	c. exotic	d. habitually	e. impartial
f. reiterate	g. simultaneous	h. urgent	i. vulnerable	j. waive

_____ 1. People who work long hours in the sun are ___ to skin cancer.

_____ 2. The ___ ringing of <u>multiple</u> church bells at noon made a lovely sound.

_____ 3. At an emergency room, patients with the most ___ problems are cared for first.

_____ 4. We have decided to ___ our right to remain silent, and so we will talk to the police.

_____ 5. Since you didn't hear me, let me ___ what I said.

_____ 6. You are a(n) ___ software writer, but we need a really excellent one for this job.

_____ 7. The ___ African language of Xhosa uses clicks for many sounds.

_____ 8. Since we can't settle the argument, let's let a(n) ___ person decide.

_____ 9. If we don't resolve the issue, this small difference of opinion might ___ into a fight.

T   F   10. People who are *habitually impartial* would make good judges.

DERIVATIONS: Write the correct word form using the choices below.

1. Because of his _____, he was <u>designated</u> for a promotion. (**competent, competence**)

2. Ignoring customer complaints often _____ problems. (**escalating, escalates**)

3. It is hard to be _____ when judging your own children. (**impartiality, impartial**)

4. Don't <u>venture</u> outside if there are _____ hurricane warnings! (**urgency, urgent**)

5. With each _____, his voice became louder. (**reiterate, reiteration**)

6. Areas of land that sit below sea level are _____ to floods. (**vulnerable, vulnerability**)

FINISH UP: Complete each sentence with a detailed phrase.

7. The *exotic* bird _____

_____.

8. *Simultaneous* with the phone call, _____

_____.

GIVE EXAMPLES: Answer with personal responses.

1. Give two examples of requirements that you would like to see *waived*.

2. Give two examples of things you *habitually* do, and briefly describe when you do them.

PASSAGE: King Tut—The Mummy's Curse

Fill in the word from each column's list that fits best.

Column 1 Choices: habitually, inquisitive, rigorous, simultaneously, terminology, waive

Column 2 Choices: assumption, cited, exotic, impartially, integrate, vulnerable

On November 25, 1922, Howard Carter <u>peered</u> through a small hole and saw a room glittering with gold. In the center was the mummy of King Tutankhamen. It was a <u>spectacular</u> discovery of ancient Egyptian treasures.

But then, according to legend, tragic things began to happen. There was a report that a cobra ate Carter's pet canary. Next, the papers related that three terrible events took place

(1) _____. At the same time, the expedition's sponsor, Lord Carnarvon, died; his dog dropped dead; and the lights went out in Cairo. Then, one by one, people on Carter's team died.

It was said that an ancient curse protected mummies. Writing, supposedly found in the tomb, read, "Death will slay with his wings whoever disturbs the peace of the pharaoh."

Today, scientists follow strict,

(2) _____ standards that protect the treasures in tombs. For this reason, explorers often leave things in place. But in those days,

workers (3) _____ disturbed things. Carter and his team took Tut's mummy and other precious things from the burial chamber. They even unwrapped the mummy to see what it looked like. The *implication* of the curse was that Carter and his team were in for trouble.

The tale of the curse grew and grew until it *escalated* into an industry. Dozens of books and movies have featured mummies who take revenge on

the (4) _____ explorers who dare to disturb tombs to find out information.

People searched for a scientific cause of the curse. In 1986, Dr. Caroline Stenger-Phillips proposed that mold found in ancient tombs might have made people sick. The medical

(5) _____ for the molds she

identified included *Aspergillus niger* and *Aspergillus flavus*. Her research publications were

(6) _____ by people who wanted to explain the mummy's curse.

But does the mummy's curse actually exist?

Let's look at the facts (7) _____, without favoring either side, to *assess* how strong the evidence for a curse is. Without investigating, many

people made the (8) _____ that the reports of deaths were accurate. But it was hard to get *precise* reporting in 1922.

In fact, it seems that it was impossible to prove when or how Carter's canary and Carnavon's dog died. Carnarvon did die six months after the discovery, but he was already in

(9) _____ health, since he had been sick for years. The lights did go out, but electric failures were common at that time. And the writing in the tomb actually read, "I am for the protection of the dead."

Finally, a *rigorous* scientific study found that the people on Carter's team did not die soon afterward. In short, there is very little evidence of a curse.

So how did it all get started? It seems that in the

1920s there was a(n) (10) _____ performance featuring women who danced around a mummy while unwrapping it. This inspired a fictional book about the mummy's curse, which became a legend.

However, perhaps it helped King Tut. Egyptians believed a person's soul would live as long as people remembered him. If this is true, King Tut's soul will live for long time.

Think About the Passage

1. According to the passage, should a *rational* person believe in the mummy's curse. Why or why not?

2. How does the treatment of mummies today differ from that in Carter's time?

PAIRS OF OPPOSITES; VALUABLE WORDS

PART 1: PAIRS OF OPPOSITES

ascend	descend	antonym	synonym	extrovert
introvert	emigrate	immigrate	optimist	pessimist

This list has five pairs of opposites. Use context clues to predict what this pair means.

Alice *ascended* to the roof of the building and admired the view. _____

When she left the roof, Alice had to *descend* several flights of stairs. _____

1. ascend (ə-sĕnd′) *verb*
   to go up
   > The hot air balloon **ascended** over the houses.
   > After winning the game, the Mavericks **ascended** to first place.
   > When the king dies, the princess will **ascend** to the throne.
   ascent *noun*   She looked out the window during the plane's *ascent*.

2. descend (dĭ-sĕnd′) *verb*
   a. to go down
   > Mom was afraid to let the baby **descend** the stairs alone.
   > After he lost his job, he **descended** into a deep depression.
   b. to come from an <u>ancestor</u> or a source from the past
   > Okpara was **descended** from a tribal chief.
   > The U.S. tradition of free speech **descends** from the country's founders.
   descendant *noun*   George Washington Carver, a *descendant* of slaves, was an agricultural chemist. (A *descendant* is a person who comes from <u>ancestors</u>.)
   descent *noun*   The plane is making its *descent*, and will soon land.

3. antonym (ăn′tə-nĭm′) *noun*
   a word that means the opposite of another word
   > The word *good* is an **antonym** of *bad*.

4. synonym (sĭn′ə-nĭm′) *noun*
   a word that means the same as another word
   > The words *excellent* and *terrific* are **synonyms**.
   > Lists of **synonyms** and <u>antonyms</u> can be found at thesaurus.com.
   synonymous *adjective*   The words *cold* and *freezing* are almost *synonymous*, but *freezing* is more intense.

> *Syn-* and *ant-* are prefixes that come at the beginning of words. *Syn-* means "the same"; *ant-* means "opposite."

5. extrovert (ĕk′strə-vûrt′) *noun*
   a social person; a person who enjoys being with others people
   > It was easy for the **extrovert** to <u>socialize</u> at parties.
   extroverted *adjective*   My *extroverted* friend enjoyed public speaking.

71

> The prefix ex- means "out."
>
> The prefix in- means "in."

6. **introvert** (ĭn′trə-vûrt′) *noun*
   a person who prefers to be alone
   > The **introvert** would rather read than attend a party.

   introverted *adjective*   Social networking allows *introverted* people to communicate with others without meeting them in person.

7. **emigrate** (ĕm′ĭ-grāt) *verb*
   to leave one country and go to live in another
   > He **emigrated** from Guatemala and went to live in Mexico.

   emigrant *noun*   The *emigrant* was homesick for the land of her birth.

8. **immigrate** (ĭm′ĭ-grāt) *verb*
   to come to another country to live
   > A 102-year-old man **immigrated** to New Zealand because England had become too crowded.

   immigrant *noun*   After five years, the *immigrant* became a citizen of his adopted land.

9. **optimist** (ŏp′tə-mĭst) *noun*
   a person who expects that good things will happen
   > The **optimist** believed that the economy would soon improve.

   optimistic *adjective*   Even though I started my assignment late, I am *optimistic* that I can finish it on time.

   optimism *noun*   My cheerful mother gave us a feeling of *optimism*.

10. **pessimist** (pĕs′ə-mĭst) *noun*
    a person who expects that the worst will happen
    > Despite good job reviews, the **pessimist** lived in fear of being fired.

    pessimistic *adjective*   The senator was *pessimistic* about the outcome of the war.

    pessimism *noun*   On election night, *pessimism* filled the room after early results made it <u>inevitable</u> that the candidate would lose.

optimist and *pessimist*

DEFINITIONS: Write the correct word for each meaning.

ascend	descend	antonym	synonym	extrovert
introvert	emigrate	immigrate	optimist	pessimist

_____ 1. a social person

_____ 2. to go down

_____ 3. to leave a country

_____ 4. a person who expects the worst

_____ 5. to go up

_____ 6. a person who likes to be alone

_____ 7. to go to live in a country

_____ 8. a person who expects the best

_____ 9. a word with the same meaning

_____ 10. a word with the opposite meaning

PART 1 EXERCISES

CONTEXT: ITEMS 1–9: Choose the best answer. **ITEM 10:** Circle true (T) or false (F).

a. ascend	b. descend	c. antonym	d. synonym	e. extrovert
f. introvert	g. emigrate	h. immigrate	i. optimist	j. pessimist

_____ 1. The word *answer* is a(n) ___ of the word *reply*.

_____ 2. I plan to _____ to Canada and live there for the rest of my life.

_____ 3. He was able to ___ from poverty to great wealth.

_____ 4. The ___ enjoyed working alone at home.

_____ 5. The ___ believed that she would quickly solve her problems.

_____ 6. If you want a career in politics, it is helpful to be a(n) ___ who enjoys meeting people.

_____ 7. The ___ always feared that he was going to flunk his tests.

_____ 8. The firemen will ___ into the basement to rescue the trapped children.

_____ 9. The word *high* is a(n) ___ of *low*.

T   F   10. People often *emigrate* from a country because they are *pessimistic* about life there.

DERIVATIONS: Write the correct word form using the choices below.

1. Research shows that sunlight contributes to _____. **(optimistic, optimism)**

2. Preferring a <u>solitary</u> life, the _____ woman avoided neighbors. **(introverted, introvert)**

3. _____ to a strange country requires adjustments. **(Immigrating, Immigrated)**

4. I plan to leave money to my _____. **(descending, descendants)**

5. The bubbles _____ into the air. **(ascending, ascended)**

6. _____ from the country of one's birth is difficult. **(Emigrating, Emigrant)**

FINISH UP: Complete each sentence with a detailed phrase.

7. **Because she was a *pessimist* _____**

_____.

8. **He searched for *synonyms* because _____**

_____.

GIVE EXAMPLES: Answer with personal responses.

9. Give two *antonyms* for the word *pretty*.

10. Describe an *extrovert* whom you know. Tell why that person is an *extrovert*.

DESCRIPTIONS: Choose the word that these examples best describe.

_____ 1. go up a mountain; go from being a worker to being a company president; a climb in a rollercoaster
    a. descend   **b.** ascend   **c.** emigrate   **d.** introvert

_____ 2. the problem of hunger will be solved; I will get a great job; I will graduate with honors
    a. extrovert   **b.** ascend   **c.** synonym   **d.** optimist

_____ 3. cold–warm; happy–sad; peaceful–warlike
    a. antonym   **b.** pessimist   **c.** introvert   **d.** synonym

_____ 4. enjoys meeting friends at restaurants; sociable; spends leisure time with other people
    a. introvert   **b.** ascend   **c.** immigrate   **d.** extrovert

_____ 5. escapes Viet Nam on a boat; leaves Syria in search of religious freedom; says good-bye to a family he will never see again
    a. introvert   **b.** emigrate   **c.** immigrate   **d.** descend

STRATEGY PRACTICE: Combining Context Clues with the Dictionary

The entries that you find in a dictionary are often complex. Here is a dictionary entry for a word on your list. Read it and then give the definition number that best fits each sentence.

---

de·scend 📢 (dĭ-sĕnd′) KEY

VERB: de·scend·ed, de·scend·ing, de·scends

1. To move from a higher to a lower place; come or go down.

2. a. To come from an ancestor or ancestry: _He was descended from a pioneer family._
    b. To come down from a source; derive: _a tradition descending from colonial days._

3. To proceed or progress downward, as in rank, pitch, or scale: _titles listed in descending order of importance; notes that descended to the lower register._

4. To arrive or attack in a sudden or an overwhelming manner: _summer tourists descending on the village._

_____ 1. The ants _descended_ on the sandwich we dropped at the picnic.

_____ 2. The mountain _descends_ into the sea.

_____ 3. The word "good-bye" _descends_ from the greeting "God be with you."

_____ 4. The list publishing test scores _descended_ from the highest score to the lowest score.

_____ 5. I am _descended_ from Navajo Native Americans.

PART 2: VALUABLE WORDS

adjacent	annul	diligent	fanatic	instigate
reciprocate	scrutinize	sibling	spontaneous	squander

This list includes a word with the prefix *ex-*, which means "out." Use context clues and the prefix meaning to predict what *exclude* means.

We do not *exclude* women from wrestling._____

11. adjacent (ə-jā′sənt) *adjective*
    next to something else

    My neighbor bought the empty lot **adjacent** to his house and built an addition.

12. annul (ə-nŭl′) *verb*
    to cancel officially; to make something not effective

    The election had so many problems that the court decided to **annul** the results and call for another vote.

    annulment *noun*   After the Pope refused to grant an *annulment* of Henry VIII's marriage, the king left the Catholic Church.

13. diligent (dĭl′ə-jənt) *adjective*
    hardworking and careful

    The **diligent** farm worker sorted berries for hours without a break.

    diligence *noun*   It requires *diligence* to check for grammatical and spelling errors.

    diligently *adverb*   She *diligently* dusted the piano every day.

14. fanatic (fə-năt′ ĭk) *noun*
    a person who is overly devoted to a cause

    The sports **fanatics** attacked women who tried to attend school.

    The sports **fanatic** screamed at anyone who interrupted him while he watched a game.

    a person who is a fan of an activity

    The crossword **fanatic** subscribed to many puzzle books.

    fanaticism *noun*   The leader's *fanaticism* in urging suicide bombings caused <u>strife</u> among his followers.

    > *Fanatic* is a negative word. *Fanatics* are more devoted to a cause than they should be, and they will not listen to reason.

15. instigate (ĭn′stĭ-gāt) *verb*
    to cause something to start

    In 2011, Egyptian Wael Ghonim **instigated** protests by sending Facebook and YouTube™ messages criticizing his government.

    The senator **instigated** tax reforms with speeches about how working people were suffering.

    instigation *noun*   At the *instigation* of parents, the school began an investigation of bullying on the playground.

16. **reciprocate** (rĭ-sĭp′rə-kāt) *verb*
    to return the feelings or actions of another person
    > I am happy to **reciprocate** your friendship.
    > My parents took care of me as a child, and I **reciprocate** by supporting them in their old age.

    reciprocation *noun*   They invited us to dinner and, in *reciprocation*, we invited them back.

17. **scrutinize** (skro͞ot′n-īz) *verb*
    to examine very carefully
    > Mom **scrutinized** each dish to make sure it was clean.
    > Every action of the U.S. president is **scrutinized** by the press.

18. **sibling** (sĭb′lĭng) *noun*
    a brother or sister
    > I am the oldest of three **siblings.**

19. **spontaneous** (spŏn-tā′nē-əs) *adjective*
    done without planning
    > The children broke out in **spontaneous** laughter when the toy popped out of its box.
    > In a **spontaneous** gesture, he grabbed his aunt and kissed her.

    spontaneously *adverb*   The group *spontaneously* burst into song.

20. **squander** (skwŏn′dər) *verb*
    to foolishly waste money or an opportunity
    > Don't **squander** your paycheck buying expensive clothes.
    > She **squandered** the chance to advance at her job by coming in late and spending time making personal calls.

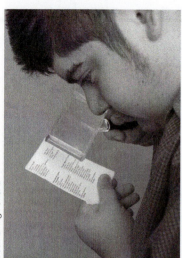

© Robert Erving Potter III

scrutinizing

A *spontaneous* person shows real feelings, rather than trying to hide them.

DEFINITIONS: Write the correct word for each meaning.

adjacent	annul	diligent	fanatic	instigate
reciprocate	scrutinize	sibling	spontaneous	squander

_____ 1. to examine very carefully

_____ 2. a person overly devoted to a cause

_____ 3. a brother or sister

_____ 4. next to

_____ 5. to cause something to start

_____ 6. done without planning

_____ 7. hardworking

_____ 8. to return feelings or actions

_____ 9. to cancel officially

_____ 10. to waste

PART 2 EXERCISES

CONTEXT: ITEMS 1–9: Choose the best answer. **ITEM 10:** Circle true (T) or false (F).

a. adjacent	b. annul	c. diligent	d. fanatic	e. instigate
f. reciprocate	g. scrutinize	h. sibling	i. spontaneous	j. squander

_____ 1. When we accidentally met on the street, we decided to have a(n) ___ dinner date.

_____ 2. Don't ___ your money on a luxury car when a basic model will meet your needs.

_____ 3. My colleague gave me a birthday gift, and I need to ___ by giving her one.

_____ 4. Inspectors will ___ the airplane to make certain it is safe to fly.

_____ 5. The ___ ordered the death of the writer who had broken religious laws.

_____ 6. My ___ and I shared a bedroom when we were children.

_____ 7. By spreading vicious gossip, the jealous woman tried to ___ trouble for her rival.

_____ 8. The court has decided to ___ that contract because it is illegal.

_____ 9. Some ___ hotel rooms have doors that connect them.

T   F   10. A *diligent* student would *squander* time listening to music, rather than finishing his paper.

DERIVATIONS: Write the correct word form using the choices below.

1. At the _____ of the domineering leader, gang members robbed a store. (**instigated, instigation**)

2. My girlfriend never _____ my feelings. (**reciprocating, reciprocated**)

3. The governor _____ the new law. (**annulled, annulment**)

4. We _____ the room, looking for bedbugs. (**scrutinizing, scrutinized**)

5. The competence and _____ of the employee earned him a raise. (**diligent, diligence**)

6. _____ opportunities does not lead to success. (**Squandering, Squander**)

FINISH UP: Complete each sentence with a detailed phrase.

7. When she won the award, she *spontaneously* _____

_____.

8. Because our desks at the office were *adjacent*. _____

_____.

GIVE EXAMPLES: Answer with personal responses.

9. Give an example of something a *fanatic* might do.

10. Give one example of why it is good to have a *sibling*.

PASSAGE: The Sixth Section—Money for Home

Fill in the word from each column's list that fits best.

Column 1 Choices: annul, emigrate, instigated, siblings, squandering, spontaneous

Column 2 Choices: adjacent, ascend, diligent, fanatics, optimism, reciprocate

If home is where the heart is, then many *immigrants* now living in Newburgh, New York, would say that Boqueron, Mexico, is their home. They will tell you

that they were forced to (1) _____ from Mexico because, in 1982, a drought destroyed their corn and bean crops. They became *pessimistic* about the possibilities of making a living in their home town, so they went to work in the United States.

The group that came to Newburgh kept in constant touch with people in Boqueron, for they

had parents, (2) _____, and even spouses there. On trips back, these *emigrants scrutinized* life in the Mexican town. They began to realize how very poor Boqueron was. A well that should have provided water was useless. Sports teams were badly equipped. It was almost impossible to get to a hospital quickly.

In New York, these people had developed rapport, and they often got together in unplanned,

(3) _____ gatherings. During their socializing, a new idea formed, although no

one is sure who (4) _____ it. They decided to create an organization called Grupo Unión to raise money for Boqueron.

Like many *immigrants* to the United States, these people saved their money rather than

(5) _____ it on buying luxuries. Most worked in low-paying jobs, as restaurant workers

or construction laborers. Although they didn't earn much, they were (6) _____ and worked hard. The ten or fifteen dollars they habitually gave each week soon added up to big changes for Boqueron.

What projects did they choose? Surprisingly, they started with a baseball stadium. Many Mexicans, like lots of people in the U.S., are sports *fanatics*. Grupo Unión felt that a stadium would give the town a feeling of pride. The organization raised $50,000 for a 2,000-person stadium.

Their next venture was to buy an ambulance. This modern vehicle could quickly

(7) _____ the hilly roads around the city to get sick people to the hospital.

Then the group raised funds for musical instruments for the band, a kitchen for the kindergarten, and a basketball court. They gave the $12,000 needed to finish the well that supplied water.

Boqueron is divided into five

(8) _____ sections, or neighborhoods. But the *emigrants* from Boqueron who moved to Newburgh have become so involved with their home town that they are now called "The Sixth Section."

The projects of the Sixth Section have given the people of Boqueron a new sense of

(9) _____ and pride. They cannot

(10) _____ by sending money to the United States, but they have given the people of Sixth Section a great feeling of satisfaction.

Think About the Passage

1. Which of the projects listed here would you have done first? Defend your answer.

2. Did the people of the Sixth Section *ascend* from poverty to wealth? Defend your answer.

QUANTITY AND QUALITY; VALUABLE WORDS

PART 1: QUANTITY AND QUALITY

accelerate	comprehensive	durable	differentiate	fraudulent
haphazard	increment	potent	surpass	utilitarian

These words describe amounts and values. Use context clues to predict what some lesson words mean.

This *durable* machine will last a long time. _____

He wants to *surpass* the world record and set a new one. _____

1. accelerate (ăk-sĕl′ə-rāt′) *verb*
    to go faster; to increase speed
    > If you press on the gas pedal, the car will **accelerate**.
    > The melting of glaciers has **accelerated** in recent years.
    acceleration *noun*   There is *acceleration* when objects fall.

    > An *accelerated class* covers material faster than a regular class.

2. comprehensive (kŏm′prĭ-hĕn′sĭv) *adjective*
    complete; covering many things
    > My **comprehensive** health insurance pays for all doctor visits.
    > The **comprehensive** program prepared us for every type of accounting work.

3. durable (dŏŏr′ə-bəl) *adjective*
    lasting or working for a long time
    > Because denim is **durable**, it is used as a fabric for work clothes.
    > The **durable** agreement kept peace in the region for fifty years.
    durability *noun*   The *durability* of stone buildings is shown by structures that are thousands of years old.

4. differentiate (dĭf′ə-rĕn′shē-āt) *verb*
    to judge differences; to show differences
    > Their mom could **differentiate** between the twins, but I couldn't.
    > The ability to get along with people often **differentiates** a good employee from a bad one.
    differentiation *noun*   The use of tones as language sounds is one point of *differentiation* between Mandarin Chinese and English.

5. fraudulent (frô′jə-lənt) *adjective*
    making a false claim; dishonest; intending to trick
    > The head of the **fraudulent** charity kept the money for himself.
    > His Ph.D. was **fraudulent**, for he had not even finished college.
    > The **fraudulent** proof of ownership fooled the bank officer into giving her a mortgage.
    fraud *verb*   It is *fraud* to cash a check that is not made out to you.

    > *Fraudulent* things are often illegal and are always meant to trick and deceive.

6. **haphazard (hăp-hăz′ərd)** *adjective*
   careless; left to chance rather than planned
   > This paper is a **haphazard** collection of sentences without logic.
   > Since they had no strategy, the army's actions were **haphazard**.
   > The box contained a **haphazard** collection of stuff.

7. **increment (ĭn′krə-mənt)** *noun*
   an increase that is one in a series
   > I get a raise of fifty dollars per week in January, followed by more **increments** in June.
   > You can add parking time on the meter in ten-minute **increments**.
   >
   > **incremental** *adjective* Instead of installing the security monitors all at once, we did it in *incremental* steps, over two months.

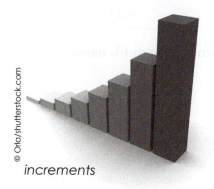

increments

8. **potent (pō′tnt)** *adjective*
   powerful; having a large effect
   > Aspirin is an <u>immensely</u> **potent** drug for reducing fever and pain.
   > The Kindle® and iPad® have been **potent** forces in changing the book industry.
   >
   > **potency** *noun*   Nuclear bombs are weapons of great **potency**.

9. **surpass (sər-păs′)** *verb*
   to go beyond
   > The U.S. budget deficit may **surpass** the legal limit.
   > My son **surpassed** my expectations when he graduated with honors.

> The word *utilitarian* comes from the word *use*.

10. **utilitarian (yōō-tĭl′ĭ-târ′ē-ən′)** *adjective*
    useful, rather than attractive
    > The **utilitarian** pots and pans were sturdy and easy to use.
    > My friends made fun of my **utilitarian** old rubber boots, but they kept my feet dry.
    >
    > **utility** *noun*   Women wear high heels because of their attractiveness, not because of their *utility*.

DEFINITIONS: Write the correct word for each meaning.

accelerate	comprehensive	durable	differentiate	fraudulent
haphazard	increment	potent	surpass	utilitarian

_____ 1. to increase speed

_____ 2. an increase

_____ 3. useful, rather than attractive

_____ 4. powerful

_____ 5. left to chance; not planned

_____ 6. to show differences

_____ 7. lasting for a long time

_____ 8. complete

_____ 9. to go beyond

_____ 10. dishonest

PART 1 EXERCISES
CONTEXT: ITEMS 1–9: Choose the best answer. **ITEM 10:** Circle true (T) or false (F).

a. accelerate	b. comprehensive	c. durable	d. differentiate	e. fraudulent
f. haphazard	g. increment	h. potent	i. surpass	j. utilitarian

_____ 1. My grandparents' ___ marriage has lasted over 50 years.

_____ 2. The price of gold is expected to ___ previous levels and reach a new high.

_____ 3. You can___ the two types of birds by the markings on their wings.

_____ 4. Hyundai introduced a(n) ___ compact car that was small and cheap to run.

_____ 5. Messy, ___ piles of paper were scattered all over the office.

_____ 6. A roller coaster will slow down as it <u>ascends</u> a track, and ___ as it goes down.

_____ 7. Every ___ in gas prices means less profit for a cab driver.

_____ 8. The ___ exam covered everything that had been taught in the course.

_____ 9. The deal was ___ because he tried to sell us a house that he didn't own.

T   F   10. A *potent* new drug for burn injuries would be expected to *accelerate* healing.

DERIVATIONS: Write the correct word form using the choices below.

1. Because of its _____, many things are made from steel. (**durable, durability**)

2. Religious belief is a force of great _____. (**potent, potency**)

3. The new machines _____ the speed of production. (**accelerated, acceleration**)

4. _____ is an important factor in selecting factory equipment. (**Utilitarian, Utility**)

5. The _____ health law adds new benefits each year (**increment, incremental**)

6. The state will prosecute you for _____. (**fraudulent, fraud**)

FINISH UP: Complete each sentence with a detailed phrase.

7. When he saw how *haphazard* our plan for the new company was, _____

_____.

8. I usually *differentiate* the games I play and the games I don't play based on _____

_____.

GIVE EXAMPLES: Answer with personal responses.

9. What would *comprehensive* car insurance cover?

10. Describe a time when you *surpassed* your own expectations.

DESCRIPTIONS: Choose the word that these examples best describe.

_____ 1. unsorted pile of clothes on the floor; disorganized junk drawer; heaps of bricks
      a. potent   **b.** haphazard   **c.** durable   **d.** differentiate

_____ 2. sorting straws by different lengths; an audition to choose who will be in a play; asking kindergarteners to put blue blocks in one pile and yellow blocks in another
      a. differentiate   **b.** comprehensive   **c.** utilitarian   **d.** fraudulent

_____ 3. a false social security card; lying on a job application; luring you to buy using devious advertising
      a. accelerate   **b.** surpass   **c.** potent   **d.** fraudulent

_____ 4. a $10 increase in your bill each month; a child increasing one shoe size each year; adding vanilla drop by drop to a cake batter
      a. haphazard   **b.** accelerate   **c.** increment   **d.** utilitarian

_____ 5. a warm, but ugly jacket; using paper towels to make coffee rather than buying expensive filters; liquid soap with no perfume in a plain bottle
      a. comprehensive   **b.** utilitarian   **c.** durable   **d.** surpass

STRATEGY PRACTICE: Combining Context Clues with the Dictionary

The entries that you find in a dictionary are often complex. Here is a dictionary entry for a word on your list. Read it and then give the part of speech and definition number for each sentence. (One answer does NOT have a definition number).

---

du·ra·ble 🔊 (door′ə-bəl, dyoor′-ə-bəl) KEY

ADJECTIVE:

1. Capable of withstanding wear and tear or decay: *a durable fabric.*

2. Lasting; stable: *a durable friendship.*

3. *Economics* Not depleted or consumed by use: *durable goods.*

NOUN: *Economics* A manufactured product, such as an automobile or a household appliance, that can be used over a relatively long period without being depleted or consumed. Often used in the plural.

OTHER FORMS:
du·ra·bil′i·ty or du′ra·ble·ness (*Noun*), **du′ra·bly** (*Adverb*)

_____ 1. Our *durable* sofa has lasted over thirty years.

_____ 2. The CEO proved to be *durable*, and he held the job for many years.

_____ 3. The U.S. manufacture of *durables* increased this month.

Houghton Mifflin Harcourt, *The American Heritage Dictionary of the English Language*, 4th ed., © 2009. Reprinted by permission.

PART 2: VALUABLE WORDS

arid	aspire	brink	browse	extinguish
hamper	intuition	persistent	reluctant	ruthless

Use context clues to predict what these lesson words mean.

The desert is an *arid* place that lacks rainfall. _____

I *aspire* to become a fashion model. _____

11. arid (ăr′ĭd) *adjective*
    a. having a very dry climate; too dry to support agriculture
       Using drip irrigation, the **arid** sands of Israel now support crop growth.
    b. dull because it lacks emotion or new ideas
       The **arid** violin performance was technically perfect, but had no passion.

12. aspire (ə-spīr′) *verb*
    to want to achieve something
       I **aspire** to be an operating room nurse.
       The professor **aspires** to have each of his students on the dean's list.
    aspiration *noun*   Her *aspirations* for being a star were realized when her
       song rose to the Top 10.

13. brink (brĭngk) *noun*
    a. the edge, especially of a high place
       Perched on the **brink** of the cliff, he could see for miles.
    b. a point of time when something is about to happen
       The cancer researchers were on the **brink** of a major discovery.
       The protests showed that Libya was on the **brink** of revolution.

A computer search *browses* for information using a *browser*. You might use Yahoo!® or Bing™ as your *browser*, for example.

14. browse (brouz) *verb*
    to look through things in a casual way
       I **browsed** through the sale items, looking for utilitarian children's clothes.
       She **browsed** through the book, reading a page here and there.

15. extinguish (ĭk-stĭng′gwĭsh) *verb*
    a. to put out a fire or a light
       Please **extinguish** your cigarette before you enter the building.
    b. to end a hope or feeling
       His need to support a family **extinguished** his hopes for college.

16. hamper (hăm′pər) *verb*
    to make something more difficult
       The many things she carried *hampered* her ability to walk quickly.
       Don't let a few problems **hamper** your efforts to succeed.

Her ability to walk quickly was *hampered*.

17. intuition (ĭn'tōō-ĭsh'ən) *noun*
    knowledge of something through feelings

    > Although the man was polite and good looking, my **intuition** told me that I should keep away from him.

    > The girl seemed to know, by **intuition**, what styles would be in fashion.

    intuitive *adjective* The salesman had an *intuitive* feeling about who would buy and who was just browsing.

Intuitive knowledge comes from feelings, and not through logic or reason.

18. persistent (pər-sĭs'tənt) *adjective*
    a. continuing to try

    > The **persistent** child kept asking if he could go in the pool.

    > If you are **persistent** enough to stay on the website, you'll get the tickets.

    b. lasting a long time

    > He finally consulted the doctor about his **persistent** cough.

    persistence *noun* Often, the key to realizing aspirations is *persistence*.
    persistently *adverb* Traffic is *persistently* a problem in big cities.
    persist *verb* If your cough *persists*, call a doctor.

19. reluctant (rĭ-lŭk'tənt) *adjective*
    unwilling; not wanting to do something

    > I am **reluctant** to cook because my family criticizes my food.

    > I forced myself to make a **reluctant** smile.

    reluctance *noun* Despite my *reluctance*, I agreed to babysit.
    reluctantly *adverb* I *reluctantly* enrolled in the difficult class.

20. ruthless (rōōth'lĭs) *adjective*
    having no pity or sense of right or wrong in achieving goals

    > The **ruthless** man stole from his mother to fund his fraudulent business scheme.

    ruthlessness *noun* We were shocked by the **ruthlessness** of the gang members who murdered anyone who got in their way.
    ruthlessly *adverb* The dictator *ruthlessly* killed his enemies.

A ruthless person will do anything to reach goals, including breaking laws and making others suffer.

DEFINITIONS: Write the correct word for each meaning.

arid	aspire	brink	browse	extinguish
hamper	intuition	persistent	reluctant	ruthless

_____ 1. to look through things in a casual way

_____ 2. to end a hope or feeling

_____ 3. to make something more difficult

_____ 4. having no pity

_____ 5. lacking in emotion or ideas

_____ 6. to want to achieve something

_____ 7. not willing

_____ 8. continuing to try

_____ 9. the edge

_____ 10. knowledge through feelings

PART 2 EXERCISES

CONTEXT: ITEMS 1–9: Choose the best answer. **ITEM 10:** Circle true (T) or false (F).

a. arid	b. aspire	c. brink	d. browse	e. extinguish
f. hamper	g. intuition	h. persistent	i. reluctant	j. ruthless

_____ 1. After three months of ___ effort, I finally succeeded.

_____ 2. The ___ man <u>habitually</u> lied, stole, cheated, and injured others.

_____ 3. The visitors were desperate to leave the country that was on the ___ of war.

_____ 4. Be sure to ___ the fire at the campsite before you leave.

_____ 5. The heavy snow will ___ our driving speed.

_____ 6. If you ___ to become a stock broker, you need to learn about financial markets.

_____ 7. When I met you, my ___ told me that we would become friends.

_____ 8. It was difficult to find fresh water in the ___ region.

_____ 9. I often ___ news websites to see what is happening.

T   F   10. If you *aspire* to become a doctor, you are *reluctant* to be in the medical profession.

DERIVATIONS: Write the correct word form using the choices below.

1. Our inability to get supplies _____ our production. **(hampering, hampered)**

2. I hope that it will be <u>feasible</u> for you to achieve your _____. **(aspires, aspirations)**

3. He _____ stole money from the homeless to buy a fancy car. **(ruthlessness, ruthlessly)**

4. I have an _____ feeling that this professor really cares. **(intuition, intuitive)**

5. Despite my _____, my <u>peers</u> convinced me to go. **(reluctance, reluctant)**

6. It takes lots of _____ to get a B.A. **(persistent, persistence)**

FINISH UP: Complete each sentence with a detailed phrase.

7. He felt he was on the *brink* of success because _____

_____.

8. We would want to *extinguish* the lights when _____

_____.

GIVE EXAMPLES: Answer with personal responses.

9. Describe an *arid* place that you have seen or know about.

10. Give an example of something that you *browse* through.

PASSAGE: Read My Face

Fill in the word from each column's list that fits best.

Column 1 Choices: brink, browse, differentiate, intuitive, reluctant, surpassed

Column 2 Choices: aspired, comprehensive, fraudulent, hampered, increment, reluctantly

Can you tell when a baby is on the

(1) _____ of tears, and about to cry? Do you recognize an expression of joy in a child's face? Of course you do! These expressions are *utilitarian,* for babies use them to communicate their needs to parents and caregivers.

The average person can interpret several expressions easily. We have a(n)

(2) _____ ability to tell, without thinking, how faces express some emotions. These include happiness, sadness, and surprise. If you

(3) _____ though pictures in a magazine, you can easily identify them. Such expressions are *durable* indicators of emotion.

But the ability to read faces is not perfect— at least for most of us. The average person

cannot (4) _____ a(n) *ruthless* person from a kind, honest person just by looking at their faces.

A few people, though, are extremely skilled. The famous psychologist Silvan Tomkins was an expert. Faces that might seem like *haphazard* combinations of muscle movements to us were *potent* signals to him. His abilities were not limited to reading

human beings. He (5) _____ his

rivals by being the best at choosing which horse would win a race. How did he do it? He interpreted the expressions on their faces!

Although he was making money <u>predicting</u>

racing winners, he (6) _____ to be a psychologist. Not surprisingly, he did research in the field of human emotions.

Following Tomkins's lead, psychologist Paul Ekman and his associates have actually put together

a(n) (7) _____ set of all human facial expressions. There are forty-six muscles in the face, and they can be combined in <u>multiple</u> ways. So the list consists of thousands of different expressions.

Facial expressions are important. There is even evidence that they can actually cause emotions. In an often <u>cited</u> experiment, people were asked to look at funny pictures. Some of them had to hold a pencil in their mouths in a way that

(8) _____ their ability to smile or laugh. These people found the pictures less funny than people who could react normally. In other words, just smiling can make you happy!

But there are different kinds of smiles. We have all seen the false smile of someone who is not really happy. It often seems to be given

(9) _____. This *arid* expression <u>conveys</u> no positive feeling, and it makes most of us uncomfortable. How can we identify it? Paul Ekman tells us that, in a real smile, we close our eyes a little, causing small creases around them. If you don't make those creases, your smile is

(10) _____.

© Darren Baker/shutterstock.com

Think About the Passage

1. How does Ekman decide if a smile is sincere?

2. Why was Tomkins good at <u>predicting</u> horse races?

3

This section will help you review the words you were taught in lessons 7, 8, and 9. It will also help you to solidify your knowledge of how to combine dictionary use with context clues.

DEFINITIONS: Fill in the letter that matches the definition of each word.

_____ 1. implication   a. to cause something to start

_____ 2. browse   b. a brother or sister

_____ 3. instigate   c. making a false claim; dishonest

_____ 4. brink   d. useful

_____ 5. competent   e. needing immediate attention

_____ 6. fraudulent   f. a hint; something not directly stated

_____ 7. fanatic   g. a feeling that you are superior to others

_____ 8. utilitarian   h. a person overly devoted to a cause

_____ 9. urgent   i. the edge

_____ 10. waive   j. not to require

     k. to look through things in a casual way

     l. capable of doing a satisfactory job

DERIVATIONS: Write the correct word form using the choices below.

1. The small oil spill is _____ into a <u>calamity</u>. **(escalated, escalation, escalating)**

2. The two words are _____. **(synonym, synonymous, synonymously)**

3. He was _____ for bravery in battle. **(citation, cite, cited)**

4. Racing cars have powerful _____. **(accelerating, accelerate, acceleration)**

5. He _____ eliminated his rivals. **(ruthless, ruthlessness, ruthlessly)**

6. The entrance exam is _____. **(rigor, rigorous, rigorously)**

7. I am the _____ of Irish immigrants. **(descend, descendant, descent)**

CONTEXT: Write in the letter of the word that best completes each sentence.
Use each choice only once.

a. arid	b. annul	c. extrovert	d. hamper
e. haphazard	f. intuition	g. optimist	h. persistent
i. precision	j. reciprocate	k. simultaneous	l. vulnerable

_____ 1. The clothes were scattered around the fitting room in a(n) ___ fashion.

_____ 2. A(n) ___ always expects that everything will be good.

_____ 3. I am a(n) ___ and I love to meet people and make new friends.

_____ 4. The storm will ___ efforts to rescue the mountain climbers.

_____ 5. The ___ little boy started to cry when his classmates made fun of him.

_____ 6. My ___ told me that I could trust her, so I told her the secret.

_____ 7. Brain surgery requires ___ because it is easy to damage tissue nearby the parts a surgeon is operating on.

_____ 8. Since she did me a favor, I would like to ___ by doing her one.

_____ 9. His constant snoring was a(n) ___, annoyance for his wife.

_____ 10. The judges will ___ the results of the race, because the winner was taking performance-enhancing drugs.

PASSAGE: Pizza Anyone?

Fill in the word from each column's list that fits best.

Column 1 Choices: aspirations, assume, habitually, immigrated, potent, reluctant, surpasses, taunt

Column 2 Choices: adjacent, assessment, comprehensive, differentiates, immense, integrated scrutinize, spontaneously

Every second, people in the U.S. eat 350 slices of pizza! A survey of children showed that pizza

(1) _____ all other foods in popularity. A full 36% of people consider it to be the perfect breakfast. In fact, 96% eat pizza

(2) _____, as one of their regular foods. Pizza has become such a popular food that its sales have become a(n)

(3) _____ force in the U.S. economy. That is to say, changes in sales levels can dramatically affect the fortunes of businesses and stock markets.

There are many huge pizza chains, but most started small. The three dots on a Dominos pizza logo stand for the three original restaurants. The high

(4) _____ and good business sense of its owners built Dominos into a nationwide chain.

Lots of people (5) _____ that pizza is a modern invention. But some form of pizza has been around for a long time. Ancient warriors once baked flat bread on shields and covered it with dates and cheese. Pizza as we know it probably originated in Naples, Italy. Italians used white sauces before explorers of the Americas brought tomatoes to Europe. When the tomato was

introduced, people were (6) _____ to use it because they thought it was poisonous. Eventually, though, they began to use tomato sauces in pizzas.

When Italians (7) _____ to the U.S., they brought pizza with them.

Pizza peddlers roamed city streets, announcing their food. Hearing their calls, workers in stores that

were (8) _____ to the street would rush out to buy lunch.

Lombardi's, the first American pizza restaurant, still operates in New York. Pizzas are produced in

coal-fired ovens. This (9) _____ them from most modern pizzas, which are made in electric ovens.

People love to judge pizza, and many blogs are

devoted to its (10) _____. Fans of

good pizza (11) _____ restaurant kitchens to make sure that ovens are exactly the right temperature and that bakers flip the dough into the air correctly.

Of course, there are many ways to top a pizza.

A (12) _____ list would include thousands of items. Have you ever eaten a pizza with chocolate chips and marshmallows, or with grapes? While some of these toppings are planned in advance, others come about when a pizza maker

(13)_____ throws some ingredients on dough. If customers like the new pizza, it is added to the menu. Pizza has been

(14) _____ into the food traditions of many countries. In Russia, a pizza may be covered a mix of sardines, tuna, mackerel, and onions. People in India use ginger, tofu, and lamb.

In short, pizza toppings offer many choices. Almost everyone can think of a favorite.

© Michael Onisiforou/shutterstock.com

STRATEGY REVIEW: Read the definitions below and use context clues to supply the letter of the definition that fits best in each sentence. Each definition is used only once.

iron
   a. a metal. (noun)
   b. great strength. (noun)
   c. irons: shackles; metal loops put around legs to prevent escape. (noun, plural)
   d. tight. (adjective)
   e. to press clothing and remove wrinkles. (verb)

_____   1. The dangerous prisoner was arrested and put in *irons*.

_____   2. When the boy tried to rob me, I held onto my wallet with an *iron* grip.

_____   3. *Iron* will rust when it is exposed to air.

_____   4. She has great self-control and a will of *iron*.

_____   5. Will you please *iron* my shirt for me?

blunt
   a. not sharp; having a dull edge. (adjective)
   b. very honest; saying exactly what one thinks. (adjective)
   c. slow to understand things; dull. (adjective)
   d. to dull an edge. (verb)
   e. to weaken; to make less effective. (verb)

_____   6. If I give you my *blunt* opinion, I am afraid I will hurt your feelings.

_____   7. If you try to cut something that is very tough, you may *blunt* the blade.

_____   8. Bushes planted around the house can *blunt* the effects of a strong wind.

_____   9. That *blunt* knife can't possibly cut the meat.

_____ 10. At times, he is a bit *blunt*, and it takes him longer to understand.

STRATEGY: PREFIXES, ROOTS, AND SUFFIXES

INTRODUCTION

In Section 4, you will study some word parts that give clues to word meanings.

WORD PARTS: PREFIXES, ROOTS, AND SUFFIXES

What is an *unpacker*? You can use the prefix, root, and suffix in this word to figure out its meaning. The word is made from several parts.

> prefix: *un-*   root: *pack*   suffix: *-er*

A **prefix** is a word part *before* the main word or root. A hyphen shows where the main word or root attaches.

A **root** is the main word part. A root can be a word, but some roots are only word parts.

A **suffix** is a word part *after* the main word or root. A hyphen shows where the main word attaches.

The prefix *un-* means "opposite" or "not."

The root *pack* is a common word.

The suffix *-er* means "a person."

So let's build the word *unpacker*. *Unpack* is the opposite of *pack*. *Pack* means to put something in; *unpack* means to take it out. An *unpacker* is a person who takes something out.

SUFFIXES: LESSON 10

You will study some common suffixes in Lesson 10. All of these suffixes add meaning to a word or word root. Three of them also perform the function of changing the part of speech.

Suffix	Meaning	Part of Speech Function	Example Words and Meanings
-er, -or	person	changes verb to noun	teach*er*—a person who teaches
-ist	person	(noun remains noun)	art*ist*—a person who creates art
-ful	filled with	changes noun to adjective	pain*ful*—filled with pain
-less	without	changes noun to adjective	pain*less*—without pain

PREFIXES: LESSONS 11 AND 12

You will study some common *prefixes* in Lessons 11 and 12. These prefixes add meaning to word roots.

Prefix	Meaning	Example Words and Meanings
non-	not	*non*sense—something that does not make sense
un-	not, opposite	*un*safe—not safe
uni-	one	*uni*directional—having one direction
bi-	two	*bi*level—having two levels
tri-	three	*tri*level—having three levels
pre-	before	*pre*test—a test taken before learning
post-	after	*post*test—a test taken after learning

MATCHING: Supply the letter that best matches the meaning of each prefix or suffix.

_____ 1. *non-*   _____ 7. *-less*

_____ 2. *tri-*   _____ 8. *un-*

_____ 3. *post-*   _____ 9. *uni-*

_____ 4. *-er*   _____ 10. *-ist*

_____ 5. *pre-*   _____ 11. *bi-*

_____ 6. *-ful*

a. full of

b. two

c. not (use this answer twice)

d. without

e. before

f. three

g. a person (use this answer twice)

h. after

i. one

SENTENCES: Write in the word that best completes each sentence.

Choices to use once: without, three, before, one, after, filled with, two
Choices to use twice: person, not

1. A person who is *unhappy* is _____ happy.

2. A *pregame* analysis takes place _____ a game.

3. A *postgame* analysis takes place _____ a game.

4. A *player* means a(n) _____ who plays.

5. A *unicycle* has _____ wheel.

6. A *bicycle* has _____ wheels.

7. A *tricycle* has _____ wheels.

8. Something *powerful* is _____ power.

9. Someone *powerless* is _____ power.

10. A *nonviolent* person is _____ violent.

11. A *terrorist* is a(n) _____ who commits terrorist acts.

SUFFIXES -ER (-OR), -IST; -FUL, -LESS

PART 1: SUFFIXES -ER (-OR), -IST

commentator	conqueror	observer	offender	performer
practitioner	biologist	conformist	meteorologist	perfectionist

When the suffixes *-er* (also spelled *-or*) and *-ist* are added to a word, they often make a new word that refers to a person. The word *jump*, for example, becomes *jumper*, which means "a person who jumps." Fill in the blanks below to practice using these suffixes.

A *performer* is a _____ who performs.

A *perfectionist* is a _____ who tries to do something perfectly.

1. **commentator** (kŏm′ən-tā′tər) *noun*   comment + -or (person)
   a person who reports, comments on, and analyzes an event
   > The **commentator** gave an analysis of the football coach's strategy.
   > A **commentator** from Syria discussed the Mideast crisis on the news.
   commentary *noun*   Blogs provide *commentary* on current events.

2. **conqueror** (kŏng′kər-ər) *noun*   conquer + -or (person)
   a person who gains control by winning military victories
   > Hernan Cortez was the **conqueror** who gained control of Mexico in the 1500s.
   conquer *verb*   Will good *conquer* evil in the movie?

3. **observer** (əb-zûr′vər) *noun*   observe + -er (person)
   a person who watches or looks
   > The United Nations sent **observers** to report on elections in Ghana.
   > **Observers** noticed that the quarterback couldn't complete passes.
   observe *verb*   I *observed* animal behavior at the zoo.

   > An *observer* looks and evaluates, but does not participate.

4. **offender** (ə-fĕn′dər) *noun*   offend + -er (person)
   a person who has committed a crime or broken a rule
   > The **offender** who robbed a store was sentenced to prison.
   > Who is the **offender** who was smoking inside the building?
   offend *verb*   Her criticism *offended* me. (*Offend* means "to upset.")

5. **performer** (pər-fôrm′ər) *noun*   perform + -er (person)
   a. a person who does something in front of an audience
   > Tickets sold out when people realized that Beyoncé would be the **performer**.
   b. a person who does something very well
   > He is an excellent **performer** in track because he has long legs and a competitive spirit.
   perform *verb*   The band will *perform* two songs.

performer

93

A practitioner works in, or practices, a profession or activity.	**6. practitioner** (prăk-tĭsh′ə-nər) *noun* **practice + -er (person)** **a.** a person who is working in a profession The nurse **practitioner** made many medical decisions. The lawyer had worked for the city, but was now a private **practitioner.** **b.** someone who regularly does an activity She is a **practitioner** of yoga.	

7. biologist (bī-ŏl′ə-jĭst) *noun* **bio (life) + -logy (study of) + -ist (person)**
a scientist who studies living things

The word biologist has two suffixes: -logy and -ist.

The **biologist** Francis Crick was one of the discoverers of the structure of DNA.

8. conformist (kən-fôr′mĭst) *noun* **conform + -ist (person)**
a person who does what most other people do

Conformist is often a negative word that refers to people who do not think for themselves.

The teenager was a **conformist** who dressed like her friends.
conform *verb* Students must *conform* to the rules.

9. meteorologist (mē′tē-ə-rŏl′ə-jĭst) *noun* **meteor (conditions in the atmosphere) + -logy (study of) + -ist (person)**
a scientist who studies and reports weather conditions

The **meteorologist** used radar to predict the hurricane's path.
meteorology *noun* Wind patterns are important to *meteorology.*

10. perfectionist (pər-fĕk′shən-ĭst) *noun* **perfect + -ion + -ist (person)**
a person who wants to do things without errors

The copy editor of a book needs to be a **perfectionist** who will correct every problem in the text.

DEFINITIONS: Write the correct word for each meaning.

commentator	conqueror	observer	offender	performer
practitioner	biologist	conformist	meteorologist	perfectionist

_____ 1. a criminal

_____ 2. person who looks at things

_____ 3. scientist who studies weather

_____ 4. person who wants to do things perfectly

_____ 5. person who does something in front of an audience

_____ 6. person who reports on events

_____ 7. person working in a profession

_____ 8. person who does what other people do

_____ 9. scientist who studies living things

_____ 10. person who gains control by military victories

PART 1 EXERCISES
CONTEXT: ITEMS 1–9: Choose the best answer. **ITEM 10:** Circle true (T) or false (F).

a. commentator	b. conqueror	c. observer	d. offender	e. performer
f. practitioner	g. biologist	h. conformist	i. meteorologist	j. perfectionist

_____ 1. Which ___ will sing first at the summer concert?

_____ 2. The ___ issued a tornado warning.

_____ 3. The ___ marched into the city he had defeated and declared victory.

_____ 4. Since everyone was going to the party, the ___ decided to go too.

_____ 5. The ___ studies wolf populations.

_____ 6. I want to be a(n) ___ who watches, but doesn't say anything.

_____ 7. He is a(n) ___ who checks his work over and over to make sure it is completely right.

_____ 8. On the business radio station, a(n) ___ gave an analysis of employment statistics.

_____ 9. This was the third time the ___ had been convicted of a crime.

T F 10. When you *observe* a trial, you are usually acting as a legal *practitioner*.

DERIVATIONS: Write the correct word form using the choices below.

1. The _____ was an analysis of the new car safety features. (**commentator, commentary**)

2. Security guards need to _____ to <u>stringent</u> guidelines. (**conform, conformity**)

3. Are you the _____ who broke the law? (**offend, offender**)

4. The _____ took notes during the court session. (**observe, observer**)

5. I want to study _____ in college. (**meteorologist, meteorology**)

6. What play is the company _____ tonight? (**performing, performed**)

FINISH UP: Complete each sentence with a detailed phrase.

7. **When the *perfectionist* washed his car,**_____

_____.

8. **A medical *practitioner*** _____

_____.

GIVE EXAMPLES: Answer with personal responses.

9. Give an example of a *conqueror,* and tell what he or she conquered.

10. Give examples of two topics a *biologist* might study.

DESCRIPTIONS: Choose the word that these examples best describe.

_____ 1. criminal; person who cheats on an exam; person who breaks into a building
   a. commentator   **b.** perfectionist   **c.** biologist   **d.** offender

_____ 2. nurse treating patients; lawyer trying a case; physician examining a boy
   a. conqueror   **b.** performer   **c.** practitioner   **d.** meteorologist

_____ 3. person making the bed again and again until the corners are precisely even; artist changing a painting until it is just the way he wants it; person altering clothing until it fits exactly
   a. perfectionist   **b.** meteorologist   **c.** conformist   **d.** observer

_____ 4. watching a game; seeing fireworks; going to a factory to see how cars are made
   a. observer   **b.** conqueror   **c.** performer   **d.** biologist

_____ 5. a women who bases her own assessments on what her friends think; a person who reads a book because it is on the best-seller list; a man who plays basketball because his buddies want him to
   a. observer   **b.** meteorologist   **c.** conqueror   **d.** conformist

STRATEGY PRACTICE: Use the suffixes -er (-or), -ist, -ful and -less.

In Part 1, you studied words with -er/-or and -ist. In Part 2, you will study words with -ful and -less.

Part 1: -er and -or mean "a person"; -ist means "a person."
Part 2: -ful means "filled with"; -less means "without."

Use these suffixes and context clues to predict the meanings of the words in italics.

1. The woman was _luckless_, and nothing seemed to go right in her life.

   Luckless means _____.

2. The _creator_ of that TV series became rich and famous.

   Creator means _____.

3. Do you think it is feasible for that _bicyclist to_ win the ten-mile race?

   Bicyclist means _____.

4. The small child took a _handful_ of cookies from the jar.

   Handful means _____.

5. Which person is the _beautifier_ who made this room look so wonderful?

   Beautifier means _____.

PART 2: SUFFIXES *-FUL, -LESS*

flavorful	flavorless	tactful	tactless	dutiful
graceful	neglectful	aimless	restless	spotless

These two suffixes are opposites. The suffix *-ful* means "filled with." The suffix *-less* means "without." Fill in the blanks below to practice using these suffixes.

Flavorful food is _____ flavor.

Water is *flavorless*, and it is _____ flavor.

11. flavorful (flā′vər-fəl) *adjective*   **flavor + -ful (filled with)**
    having lots of taste; delicious
    Cooking a stew slowly makes it more **flavorful.**

> *Flavorful* usually refers to foods that are **not** sweet.

12. flavorless (flā′vər-lĭs) *adjective*   **flavor + -less (without)**
    lacking in flavor; lacking taste
    Canned peas are **flavorless** compared to fresh ones.
    The liquid vitamins are **flavorless.**

13. tactful (tăkt′fəl) *adjective*   **tact + -ful (filled with)**
    expressing opinions in ways that do not upset people
    The **tactful** professor described the failing paper as "needing improvement."
    It is **tactful** to agree with your boss in public.
    tactfulness, tact *noun*   Thanks for your *tactfulness* (*tact*) in this matter.

14. tactless (tăkt′lĭs) *adjective*   **tact + -less (without)**
    expressing opinions in ways that upset other people
    The **tactless** professor <u>bluntly</u> described the failing paper as the worst assignment she had ever seen.
    His **tactless** remarks about the food hurt the hostess's feelings.
    tactlessness *noun*   Your *tactlessness* is shocking.

15. dutiful (dōō′tĭ-fəl) *adjective*   **duty + -ful (filled with)**
    carefully fulfilling obligations and tasks
    The **dutiful** son took care of his sick mother.
    dutifully *adverb*   The religious man *dutifully* recited prayers.

> Note that the *y* in *duty* changes to *i* in *dutiful*.

16. graceful (grās′fəl) *adjective*   **grace + -ful (filled with)**
    a. smooth and attractive in movement
       We admired the **graceful** moves of the flamenco dancer.
    b. beautiful in shape or form
       The **graceful** sculptures add to the charm of the garden.
    gracefulness *noun*   The *gracefulness* of the woman's movements helped her to be a successful model.

graceful movement

© Andy-pix/shutterstock.com

17. neglectful (nĭ-glĕkt′fəl) *adjective*   neglect + -ful (filled with)
    not giving care or attention
        The **neglectful** officials haven't inspected our elevator in ten years.
        The mother was so **neglectful,** that the state took custody of her children.
    neglect *verb*   Don't *neglect* your homework!
    neglect *noun*   The dilapidated house suffered from *neglect.*

18. aimless (ām′lĭs) *adjective*   aim + -less (without)
    having no plan; lacking purpose
        He spent his **aimless** life listening to songs on his iPod®.
    aimlessly *adverb*   They walked *aimlessly*, without any sense of where they
        were going.

19. restless (rĕst′lĭs) *adjective*   rest + -less (without)
    a. not able to keep still
        I spent a **restless** night trying to position myself in bed, so that the
        persistent pain would go away.
        Children become **restless** when they have to sit for a long time.
    b. wanting change because you are not satisfied
        My lack of vacations at work made me **restless** to find another job.
    restlessness *noun*   One symptom of attention deficit disorder is *restlessness.*

20. spotless (spŏt′lĭs) *adjective*   spot + -less (without)
    a. perfectly clean
        There was not a speck of dust in her **spotless** house.
    b. perfectly honest
        He has a **spotless** reputation because he always does the right thing.

DEFINITIONS: Write the correct word for each meaning.

flavorful	flavorless	tactful	tactless	dutiful
graceful	neglectful	aimless	restless	spotless

_____ 1. not able to keep still

_____ 2. upsetting people with
   your opinions

_____ 3. delicious

_____ 4. not giving care or
   attention

_____ 5. carefully doing
   obligations

_____ 6. perfectly clean

_____ 7. lacking purpose

_____ 8. smooth and attractive

_____ 9. NOT upsetting people
   with your opinions

_____ 10. lacking taste

PART 2 EXERCISES

CONTEXT: ITEMS 1–9: Choose the best answer. **ITEM 10:** Circle true (T) or false (F).

| a. flavorful | b. flavorless | c. tactful | d. tactless | e. dutiful |
| f. graceful | g. neglectful | h. aimless | i. restless | j. spotless |

_____ 1. Because it is ___, you will not be able to taste the food coloring in the cake.

_____ 2. The plants died when the ___ owner forgot to water them.

_____ 3. His ___ remarks about his wife's haircut hurt her feelings.

_____ 4. We admired the ___, flowing movements of the swimmer.

_____ 5. He is a(n) ___ person, who doesn't seem to have any goals in life.

_____ 6. She spent hours cleaning the apartment until it was ___.

_____ 7. The chicken dish was so ___ that we asked mom to make it again soon.

_____ 8. Sitting on the sofa made me _____, so I got up and walked around the room.

_____ 9. The ___ parent attended all of his son's school conferences.

T   F   10. A *tactful* person would be *neglectful* of other people's feelings.

DERIVATIONS: Write the correct word form using the choices below.

1. We admired the _____ of the birds' flight. (**graceful, gracefulness**)

2. We wandered _____ through the immense mall. (**aimless, aimlessly**)

3. Your _____ helped your colleagues avoid a fight at the meeting. (**tactful, tact**)

4. The man's _____ annoyed the people who were sitting nearby. (**restless, restlessness**)

5. I _____ reported for work each morning at 7 AM. (**dutiful, dutifully**)

FINISH UP: Complete each sentence with a detailed phrase.

6. **I find this fruit *flavorless*, so** _____

_____.

7. **The *tactless* remark he made was** _____

_____.

8. **If you are *neglectful* of your studies,** _____

_____.

GIVE EXAMPLES: Answer with personal responses.

9. Give two examples of foods you consider to be *flavorful*.

10. Give an example of a place or a thing that needs to be *spotless*.

PASSAGE: Weather Wise

Fill in the word from each column's list that fits best.

Column 1 Choices: biologists, conquer, gracefully, neglectful, offender, spotless

Column 2 Choices: commentator, flavorful, meteorologist, perfectionist, practitioners, restless

The weather affects every living thing. Tornados may be beautiful to watch as they move

(1) _____ through the sky, but the damage they cause can take years to repair.

Weather events have had important <u>effects</u> on history. In 1588, Spain invaded England, hoping to

(2) _____ it. Unfortunately, a storm at sea destroyed Spanish ships, ruining their plans. Weather also played a part in the American Revolution. In 1776, George Washington's army was trapped by the British on Long Island. But a fog rolled in and helped the Americans escape to Manhattan.

Weather has <u>effects</u> on animal populations too.

We have been warned by (3) _____ that warming weather is causing problems for polar bears and deer. A new pest called the "stink bug" is expected to come to the U.S. as temperatures rise.

The weather also affects the small things we do. Perhaps, *neglecting* to listen to weather forecasts, you washed your car, only to find the

(4) _____ shine ruined a few hours later by rain.

People have tried to change the weather. Thousands of years ago our <u>ancestors</u> felt that they had to please the gods to get good weather. They believed that if

they were (5) _____ and forgot to offer prayer or sacrifices, they would be punished. To put it very *tactfully*, such methods were not scientific!

However, people are still trying to change weather. One scheme includes pouring soapy water over the sea in the path of a hurricane to <u>hamper</u> the winds. So far, though, such strategies have not been successful.

In fact, we cannot even <u>predict</u> weather very well. As many *observers* have noted, weather forecasts are not always accurate. Weather forecasting is an activity that would not be suited

to a (6) _____!

However, advances are making prediction better and better. A trained (7) _____ is a highly skilled individual. Many have Ph.D.s.

The (8) _____ who are involved in weather prediction use sophisticated tools, including ceilometers (to measure cloud height), wind anemometers (for speed), and aneroid barometers (for air pressure). They often are involved in computer modeling and use precise <u>terminology</u>.

But what about the people you see reporting the weather each night on TV? Often they have no formal training. These people may simply be *performers* who *dutifully* read the weather reports that are

given to them. Perhaps your local weather reporter

was once a fashion (9) _____ who became tired of her job. Seeing that she was

(10) _____, the station put her in charge of the weather. On the other hand, some weather reporters are very well trained.

Perhaps in the future, we will be able to predict the weather accurately, and even to control it. In the meantime, though, we will be governed by the powerful and unpredictable forces that shape nature.

Think About the Passage

1. Identify one way in which weather has affected human history.

2. Give an example of why the weather is of interest to *biologists*.

PREFIXES NON-; UN-

PART 1: THE PREFIX NON-

nonappearance	nonassertive	noncompetitive	noncompliant	nonflammable
nonhazardous	noninvasive	nonjudgmental	nonrecurring	nonstandard

Prefixes are added before a root or a word. The prefix *non-* means "not." Fill in the blank below to practice using this prefix.

A *noninvasive* medical test does _____ invade the body.

The *nonstandard* floor boards were _____ standard in size.

1. nonappearance (nŏn′ə-pîr′əns) *noun*   non- (not) + appear + -ance
not appearing when you have been ordered or are expected

> Because of the accused man's **nonappearance** in court, the judge ordered his arrest.

> After the protests began, the dictator pursued a policy of **nonappearance** and would not speak in public.

Nonappearance often refers to legal situations in courts of law.

2. nonassertive (nŏn′ə-sûr′tĭv) *verb*   non- (not) + assert + -ive
not aggressive; not speaking to give your views

> The coach was **nonassertive** at the meeting, but we all knew that he controlled the team.

> If you are **nonassertive** we will not know how you feel.

3. noncompetitive (nŏn′kəm-pĕt′ĭ-tĭv) *adjective*   non- (not) + compete + -ive
a. not involving competition; not involving winning and losing

> The card game was so **noncompetitive** that we didn't even keep score.

b. not able to compete; not able to win

> Your prices are so high that your store is **noncompetitive**.

> New employees sign a **noncompetitive** agreement that forbids them from working for rival companies for five years after they leave this one.

4. noncompliant (nŏn′kəm-plī′ənt) *adjective*   non- (not) + comply + -ant
not obeying orders or directions

> Mentally ill people are often **noncompliant** in taking medicines.

noncompliance *noun*   The regulation states that there is a $500 fine for *noncompliance* in registering a gun.

5. nonflammable (nŏn-flăm′ə-bəl) *adjective*   non- (not) + flame + -able
not able to burn

> Candles should be placed in **nonflammable** containers.

6. **nonhazardous** (nŏn-hăz′ər-dəs) *noun*   **non-** (not) + **hazard** + **-ous**
not dangerous
The materials in the toy are **nonhazardous** and will not injure your baby.

A pill that is swallowed enters the body, but is *noninvasive* because body tissue is not disturbed. In contrast, drawing blood breaks the skin, and is invasive.

7. **noninvasive** (nŏn′ĭn-vă′sĭv) *adjective*   **non-** (not) + **invade** + **-ive**
not entering the body and breaking tissues
Taking a pulse is a **noninvasive** procedure, which can be done simply by laying a finger on someone's wrist.

8. **nonjudgmental** *verb* (nŏn′jŭj-mĕn′tl) *adjective*   **non-** (not) + **judgment** + **-al**
not judging other people
A **nonjudgmental** marriage counselor will not determine blame, but instead will be <u>impartial</u> and try to improve the relationship.

9. **nonrecurring** (nŏn-rĭ-kûr′ĭng) *adjective*   **non-** (not) + **recur** + **ing**
not happening again; likely to occur only once
The **nonrecurring** tax had to be paid only in 2012.

10. **nonstandard** (nŏn-stăn′dərd) *adjective*   **non-** (not) + **standard**
not a standard type, size, or form of speech
The custom-made truck required **nonstandard** tires that had to be specially ordered.
Nonstandard expressions like *yep* should be avoided in job interviews.
The word *ain't* is an example of **nonstandard** speech.

© Robert Erving Potter III

nonstandard-sized boards

DEFINITIONS: Write the correct word for each meaning.

nonappearance	nonassertive	noncompetitive	noncompliant	nonflammable
nonhazardous	noninvasive	nonjudgmental	nonrecurring	nonstandard

_____ 1. not showing up or appearing

_____ 2. not obeying orders

_____ 3. not aggressive

_____ 4. not dangerous

_____ 5. not breaking tissues in the body

_____ 6. not standard

_____ 7. happening only once

_____ 8. not involving winning or losing

_____ 9. not able to burn

_____ 10. not evaluating other people

PART 1 EXERCISES

CONTEXT: ITEMS 1–9: Choose the best answer. **ITEM 10:** Circle true (T) or false (F).

a. nonappearance	b. nonassertive	c. noncompetitive	d. noncompliant	e. nonflammable
f. nonhazardous	g. noninvasive	h. nonjudgmental	i. nonrecurring	j. nonstandard

_____ 1. I am sure this is a ___ activity, and that it is safe for children to participate.

_____ 2. Research is developing ___ methods to monitor diabetes without drawing blood.

_____ 3. The employee was so ___ that he never spoke in meetings.

_____ 4. Slang words like *yo* are examples of ___ English.

_____ 5. His ___ comment did not tell me whether he thought my paper was good or bad.

_____ 6. Water cannot catch on fire, so it is a ___ liquid.

_____ 7. The ___ private in the army refused to obey the sergeant's orders.

_____ 8. Since you will need to pay for this only once, it is a ___ expense.

_____ 9. T-ball is a(n) ___ game, with no winners or losers.

T   F   10. A *nonappearance* by a person who has been ordered to come to court is *noncompliant*.

FINISH UP: Complete each sentence with a detailed phrase.

1. I prefer *noninvasive* medical procedures to invasive procedures because _____

   _____.

2. The *noncompliant* employee _____

   _____.

3. She wished she had bought a *nonflammable* tablecloth when _____

   _____.

4. Because of the *nonappearance* of the person who was supposed to speak at the dinner, _____

   _____.

GIVE EXAMPLES: Answer with personal responses.

5. Give an example of something you hope will be *nonrecurring*.

6. Give two examples of *nonstandard* English words or expressions.

7. Give an example of an activity that is *noncompetitive*.

8. Give an example of a time that it is good to be *nonjudgmental*.

9. Give an example of an activity that is *nonhazardous*.

10. Give an example of a time you were *nonassertive*.

DESCRIPTIONS: Choose the word that these examples best describe.

_____ 1. material that is not dangerous; good conditions on the highway; safe place in a storm
  a. nonappearance   b. nonhazardous   c. nonstandard   d. noncompliant

_____ 2. being born; dying; buying the only house you will ever own
  a. noninvasive   b. nonrecurring   c. nonflammable   d. nonstandard

_____ 3. no contests; your brothers and sisters cooperating with you; everyone gets a prize
  a. noncompetitive   b. nonstandard   c. nonappearance   d. nonflammable

_____ 4. skipping practice; not going to class; not showing up for a party you say you will come to
  a. nonappearance   b. nonassertive   c. noninvasive   d. nonstandard

_____ 5. not wearing the required name tag; breaking the coach's rules for practice; refusing to do the exercises that your physical therapist prescribes
  a. nonjudgmental   b. nonhazardous   c. noninvasive   d. noncompliant

STRATEGY PRACTICE: Use the prefixes _non-_ and _un-_.

In Part 1, you studied words with _non-_. In Part 2 you will study words with _un-_.

  Part 1: _Non-_ means "not"
  Part 2: _Un-_ means "not" or "opposite"

Use these prefixes and context clues to predict the meanings of the words in italics.

1. These towels are _nonabsorbent,_ and they won't soak up the water we spilled.

   Nonabsorbent means _____.

2. He was born in China, but he grew up here, so he speaks _unaccented_ English.

   Unaccented means _____.

3. I have two dependent children that I support, and two _nondependent_ children.

   Nondependent means _____.

4. The champion team proved to be _unbeatable._

   Unbeatable means _____.

5. Digging into the ground, the construction worker accidently _unearthed_ buried treasure.

   Unearthed means _____.

PART 2: THE PREFIX *UN-*

unaccustomed	unappetizing	unbecoming	unconventional	undocumented
unfounded	unprincipled	unrest	unruly	unsettling

The prefix *un-* can mean "not" or "opposite." Fill in the blank to practice using this prefix.

Something unappetizing is _____ appetizing.

11. **unaccustomed** (ŭn′ə-kŭs′təmd) *adjective*   un- (not) + accustom + -ed
    not doing something as a habit; not used to something
    > I was **unaccustomed** to sleeping on the floor, so I spent a restless night.
    > He was nervous because he was **unaccustomed** to speaking publicly.

12. **unappetizing** (ŭn-ăp′ĭ-tī′zĭng) *adjective*   un- (not) + appetize + -ing
    not appealing in flavor or appearance
    > The **unappetizing** bread was a shapeless brown mass.
    > I refused his **unappetizing** offer of a cold shower.

Unappetizing can refer to things that are not food.

13. **unbecoming** (ŭn′bĭ-kŭm′ĭng) *adjective*   un- (not) + become + ing
    a. not flattering; not making someone look good
    > Dad thought Ayesha's prom dress was **unbecoming.**
    b. not suitable; not appropriate
    > His frequent temper tantrums were **unbecoming** to his position as
    >   president of a large company.
    becoming *adjective*   The color red is very *becoming* to me.

14. **unconventional** (ŭn′kən-vĕn′shə-nəl) *noun*   un- (not) + convention + -al
    not ordinary or usual
    > Motown Records' **unconventional** ways of making clapping sounds
    >   included banging wooden sticks and pots.
    > Instead of saying "hello," the man gave us the **unconventional** greeting
    >   of "May the force be your guide."
    <u>**conventional**</u> *adjective*   "Hi" is a *conventional* greeting.

15. **undocumented** (ŭn-dŏk′yə-mĕn′tĭd) *adjective*   un- (not) + document + -ed
    not supported by official papers or documents
    > What is the source of the **undocumented** references in your research paper?
    > Canadian officials were concerned about **undocumented** farm laborers.

Undocumented workers or residents often refer to people who do not have official permission to stay in a country.

16. **unfounded** (ŭn-foun′dĭd) *adjective*   un- (not) + found + -ed
    not based on evidence; having no basis
    > Her suspicions about her boyfriend were **unfounded,** for he had always
    >   been true to her.
    > The rumors that the company was bankrupt were **unfounded.**

17. **unprincipled** (ŭn-prĭn′sə-pəld) *adjective*   **un- (not) + principle + -ed**
immoral; dishonest; lacking principles
> The **unprincipled** judge decided cases in favor of people who bribed him.

> **principled** *adjective*   The *principled* judge was always fair.

18. **unrest** (ŭn-rĕst′) *noun*   **un- (not) + rest**
a troubled political situation, often with protests and violence
> Marches protesting government policies contributed to **unrest** in the city.

> Social **unrest** increases when people can't find jobs.

19. **unruly** (ŭn-rōō′lē) *adjective*   **un- (not) + rule + -ly**
difficult to control or rule
> The substitute teacher couldn't get the **unruly** children to behave.

> No matter how much I comb it, my **unruly** hair kept sticking up.

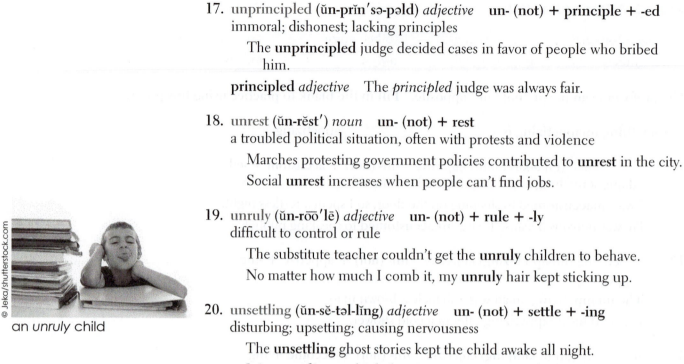

an *unruly* child

20. **unsettling** (ŭn-sĕ-təl-lĭng) *adjective*   **un- (not) + settle + -ing**
disturbing; upsetting; causing nervousness
> The **unsettling** ghost stories kept the child awake all night.

> It is **unsettling** to think that immense amounts of aid money intended for food and medicine is wasted.

DEFINITIONS: Write the correct word for each meaning.

unaccustomed	unappetizing	unbecoming	unconventional	undocumented
unfounded	unprincipled	unrest	unruly	unsettling

_____ 1. not ordinary or usual

_____ 2. not appealing

_____ 3. a troubled political situation

_____ 4. not used to something

_____ 5. not supported by official documents

_____ 6. disturbing

_____ 7. not based on evidence

_____ 8. difficult to control

_____ 9. not making someone look good

_____ 10. dishonest

PART 2 EXERCISES

CONTEXT: ITEMS 1–9: Choose the best answer. **ITEM 10:** Circle true (T) or false (F).

a. unaccustomed	b. unappetizing	c. unbecoming	d. unconventional	e. undocumented
f. unfounded	g. unprincipled	h. unrest	i. unruly	j. unsettling

_____ 1. I was surprised that my grandma's birth was ___, and no record existed of it.

_____ 2. The ___ man stole money from the club treasury.

_____ 3. The family refused to eat the ___ mess that dad cooked.

_____ 4. The choir leader could not get the ___ children to quit talking and start singing.

_____ 5. I am ___ to living alone, for I have always lived with my family.

_____ 6. That ___ rumor about his quitting school has no basis in fact.

_____ 7. The <u>persistent</u> public protests showed that there was much political ___ in the country.

_____ 8. At one time, it was ___ for women to be lawyers and doctors, but now it is common.

_____ 9. That hat is ___ to you, and I don't think you should buy it.

T   F   10. The news that a person whom you trusted was *unprincipled* would be *unsettling*.

DERIVATIONS: Write the correct word form using the choices below.

1. He is a _____ person with a <u>profound</u> sense of honor. (**principled, unprincipled**)

2. It is _____ for a college student to shout and scream. (**becoming, unbecoming**)

3. The _____ man often did things differently. (**conventional, unconventional**)

FINISH UP: Complete each sentence with a detailed phrase.

4. I am *unaccustomed* to _____

_____.

5. The *unruly* apartment renters _____

_____.

6. Because my purchase was *undocumented* by the store, _____

_____.

GIVE EXAMPLES: Answer with personal responses.

7. Give an example of three foods you consider *unappetizing*.

8. Give an example of news that you would find *unsettling*, and tell why.

9. Give an example of an *unfounded* rumor. You may create one.

10. Give an example of political *unrest* in a country.

PASSAGE: Weddings Weird and Wonderful

Fill in the word from each column's list that fits best.

Column 1 Choices: noncompliance, noninvasive, unfounded, unappetizing, unbecoming, undocumented

Column 2 Choices: nonassertive, noncompetitive, nonjudgmental, unprincipled, unrest, unsettling

Weddings are events with traditions. Most of us are familiar with bridal gowns, <u>reciprocal</u> giving of rings, and an <u>escorted</u> walk down the aisle. But other cultures have customs that seem *unconventional* to us.

In the past, many of these customs remained

(1) _____ because reporters were unable to travel to faraway locations. But as communication improves, we are learning about them.

In Scotland, people traditionally "blacken the

bride." A smelly and (2) _____ mixture of eggs, sausage, butter, cheese, and fish is poured over her. Those *unaccustomed* to seeing this might think the bride is being attacked in some <u>bizarre</u> fashion. Instead it is meant to bring good luck to the marriage.

Feet washing is another old Scottish custom. Single friends wash the bride's feet in a bowl. Before they start, a married woman puts her ring into the water. Legend says that a single woman who finds the ring will be married next. Of course, this is a(n)

(3) _____ superstition that has no basis in fact. However, it is equally silly to believe, as some of us do, that the person who catches the bouquet at a wedding will be soon be married.

In Malaysia, traditional members of the Tidong tribe require newlyweds not to use the bathroom for 72 hours. Relatives watch them to guard against

(4) _____.

Women of the Lahu people, who live in China, shave off their hair after being married, leaving only a lock on the top. Although we would find this

(5) _____ to their appearance, The Lahu believe that baldness is clean and attractive.

Unmarried girls from the Gelao tribe, also located in China, often knock out a tooth or two. This

is to make sure that (6) _____ young men who might want to attack them, will find them less appealing.

Crying is common at weddings. But many people find the huge amount of tears in the Chinese Tujia

tribe to be (7) _____ and disturbing. The future bride and her relatives are required to cry for a month. A Crying Song is sung at the wedding. This is surely a *nonstandard* way to celebrate a happy occasion.

Weddings are so important in Tajikistan that families have gone into debt trying to outdo each other. The government has passed laws in an effort to

make weddings more (8) _____. They are now limited to three hours, 150 guests, and one main course. BBC reporters covered one such Tajik wedding. The day of the occasion, the village was wired for electricity. Women are supposed to be

(9) _____, so the bride was hidden behind a curtain.

These customs are specific to their cultures, and

we should remain (10) _____ about them. After all, we also do some strange things at weddings.

But there are some things that are true for every wedding. The *nonappearance* of a bride or groom is a disaster. And we hope that a wedding will be a *nonrecurring* event. For doing it again would be the result of a divorce or death.

Think About the Passage

1. What do you think is the most *unconventional* wedding custom in the passage?

2. Which custom involves the most *unruly* behavior? Why do you think so?

PREFIXES UNI-, BI-, TRI-; PRE-, POST-

PART 1: PREFIXES UNI-, BI-, TRI-

uniformity	unique	unison	universal	bifocals
bilingual	bisect	triathlon	trilingual	triple

These prefixes signal numbers. *Uni-* means "one"; *bi-* means "two"; and *tri-* means "three." Fill in the blanks below to practice them.

Uniformity means things are done _____ way.

To *bisect* something means to divide it into _____ parts.

A *triathlon* has _____ events.

1. **uniformity** (yoo-nə-fôrm′ĭ-tē′) *noun*   uni- (one) + form + -ity
   the condition of being the same
   > The **uniformity** of airport security procedures helps to ensure our safety.
   > The religious rulers demanded **uniformity** of belief.
   uniform *adjective*   At work, we are evaluated in a *uniform* manner.

   > The noun *uniform* is also specific clothing that everyone must wear. There is *one* way of dressing.

2. **unique** (yoo-nēk′) *adjective*   uni- (one)
   a. being the only one
   > This valuable stamp is **unique**; there is no other like it.
   b. the best; having no equal
   > Author Dr. Seuss had a **unique** ability to create nonsense that children loved.
   uniquely *adverb*   I love those *uniquely* designed perfume bottles.

3. **unison** (yoo′nĭ-sən) *noun*   uni- (one) + sonus (sound)
   something everyone does at the same time
   > The choir members could not sing in **unison**, no matter how hard they tried.
   > The soldiers marched in **unison**.

4. **universal** (yoo-nə-vûr′səl) *adjective*   uni- (one) + vers (turn) + -al
   applying to everything or everyone
   > The need for food and water is **universal** among human beings.
   > Do U.S. citizens support **universal** health care?
   universally *adverb*   It is *universally* true that animals need oxygen.
   universe *noun*   The center of our *universe* is the sun.

   > The origin of this word is taken from the fact that the *universe* "turns" as one thing.

5. bifocals (bī-fō′kəl, bī′fō-kəl) *noun, plural*   bi- (two) + focus + -s
   lenses that correct vision in two different ways
   > The top part of these **bifocals** gives me the ability to see far away, and the bottom lenses enable me to read.

   bifocal *adjective*   The line in grandma's glasses marks the *bifocal* division.

bisected melon

6. bilingual (bĭ-lĭng′gwəl) *adjective*   bi- (two) + lingua (language)
   speaking two languages
   > Sibel is **bilingual** in Turkish and English.
   > The **bilingual** children's book had text in English and Spanish.

   bilingualism *noun*   In Switzerland, *bilingualism* is common.

7. bisect (bī′sĕkt′) *verb*   bi- (two) + sect (cut)
   to divide into two equal parts
   > We **bisected** the piece of pie, and gave half to each child

8. triathlon (trī-ăth′lən) *noun*   tri- (three) + decathlon (an athletic contest with several events)
   an athletic event involving three different parts
   > Most **triathlons** involve swimming, cycling, and running.

9. trilingual (trī-lĭng′gwəl) *adjective*   tri- (three) + lingua (language)
   speaking three languages
   > Mamed is **trilingual** in Azeri, Russian, and English.

10. triple (trĭp′əl)   tri- (three) + plus (fold)
    a. *adjective* consisting of three things
       > They won the exciting game in **triple** overtime.
    b. *verb* to multiply by three
       > We need to **triple** the amount of food we ordered because we expect three times as many guests.

DEFINITIONS: Write the correct word for each meaning.

| uniformity | unique | unison | universal | bifocals |
| bilingual | bisect | triathlon | trilingual | triple |

_____ 1. the condition of being the same

_____ 2. being the only one

_____ 3. glasses with two different corrections

_____ 4. consisting of three things

_____ 5. speaking three languages

_____ 6. speaking two languages

_____ 7. an athletic contest of three events

_____ 8. something everyone does at the same time

_____ 9. applying to everyone or everything

_____ 10. to divide into two equal parts

PART 1 EXERCISES

CONTEXT: ITEMS 1–9: Choose the best answer. **ITEM 10:** Circle true (T) or false (F).

a. uniformity	b. unique	c. unison	d. universal	e. bifocals
f. bilingual	g. bisect	h. triathlon	i. trilingual	j. triple

_____ 1. When the speaker asked people to respond, everyone said "yes" in ___.

_____ 2. Since everyone was dressed in black at the funeral, there was a ___ of color.

_____ 3. My ___ mother speaks Polish and English.

_____ 4. Can you draw a line that will ___ the circle into two halves?

_____ 5. Sleep is a ___ need for all human beings.

_____ 6. I am so hungry that I want a(n) ___ serving of fried chicken.

_____ 7. I am ___ in Polish, Russian, and English.

_____ 8. Since the jeweler only made one bracelet like this, it is ___.

_____ 9. His old glasses had only one correction, but his new ___ have two.

T   F   10. *Uniform* requirements would help keep the *triathlon* fair.

DERIVATIONS: Write the correct word form using the choices below.

1. She could <u>differentiate</u> two colors, but the paint color looked _____ to me. (**uniform, uniformity**)

2. This court reporting job requires _____ in English and Spanish. (**bilingualism, bilingual**)

3. I feel that I am _____ qualified to be a wedding planner. (**unique, uniquely**)

4. Mother Teresa is _____ admired for her work with the poor. (**universe, universally**)

5. I am <u>unaccustomed</u> to needing a _____ correction. (**bifocal, bifocals**)

6. A yellow line _____ the road. (**bisect, bisects**)

FINISH UP: Complete each sentence with a detailed phrase.

7. It is good for a group of people to speak in *unison* when _____

_____.

8. If I were *trilingual*, I would want to speak _____

_____.

GIVE EXAMPLES: Answer with personal responses.

9. Give an example of a *triple*-digit temperature.

10. Give an example of events that might be in a *triathlon*.

DESCRIPTIONS: Choose the word that these examples best describe.

_____ 1. everyone having the same opinion; people all voting the same way; one type of electric plug used by everyone
   a. triple   **b.** uniformity   **c.** unison   **d.** bisect

_____ 2. three people; multiply by three; rule changes involving grades, attendance, and entrance
   a. bilingual   **b.** trilingual   **c.** triple   **d.** unique

_____ 3. everybody shouts at the same time; singing together; a robbery makes four alarms go off at once
   a. triple   **b.** unison   **c.** uniformity   **d.** unique

_____ 4. a book written in French, English, and Spanish; a person who speaks Swahili, Arabic, and French; a movie in French and German with subtitles in Japanese.
   a. uniformity   **b.** bilingual   **c.** bifocals   **d.** trilingual

_____ 5. the need for people to breathe; water being wet; month-old babies that cannot talk
   a. unison   **b.** bisect   **c.** universal   **d.** triathlon

STRATEGY PRACTICE: Use the prefixes _uni-, bi-, tri-, pre-,_ and _post-._

In Part 1, you studied words with _uni-, bi-,_ and _tri-._ In Part 2, you will study words with _pre-_ and _post-._

Part 1: _Uni-_ means "one." _Bi-_ means "two." _Tri-_ means "three."
Part 2: _Pre-_ means "before." _Post-_ means "after."

Use these prefixes and context clues to predict the meanings of the words in italics.

1. When you get health insurance, you need to report _preexisting_ conditions.

   Preexisting means _____.

2. Make sure you don't go the wrong way on this _unidirectional_ road.

   Unidirectional means _____.

3. The _tricornered_ hat was in fashion in the 1700s.

   Tricornered means _____.

4. My family is _bicultural_ because they came from Egypt, but have adapted to Mexican society.

   Bicultural means _____.

5. During the _postelection_ week, <u>commentators</u> analyzed the results.

   Postelection means _____.

PART 2: PREFIXES *PRE-, POST-*

precede	prehistoric	premonition	prescription	preoperative
postoperative	posterity	posthumous	postpone	postseason

The prefix *pre-* means "before." The prefix *post-* has the opposite meaning of "after." Fill in the blanks below to practice using these prefixes.

Preoperative care is given _____ an operation.

Postoperative care is given _____ an operation.

11. **precede** (prĭ-sēd′) *verb* pre- (before) + cede (to come)
    to come before
    > The month of March **precedes** the month of April.
    > A very slow person **preceded** me in the buffet line.

12. **prehistoric** (prē′hĭ-stôr′ĭk) *adjective* pre- (before) + history + -ic
    referring to a time in the past before writing was used
    > **Prehistoric** art gives us information about ancient humans.

13. **premonition** (prē′mə-nĭsh′ən, prĕm′ə-nĭsh′ən) *noun* pre- (before) + monere (warn) + -ion
    a. a feeling that something is about to happen
    > I had a **premonition** that I would have a bad day.
    b. a warning
    > His serious voice was a **premonition** of bad news.

14. **prescription** (prĭ-skrĭp′shən) *verb* pre- (before) + script (write) + -ion
    a. a written note from a physician required before getting medication
    > Do you need a **prescription** for aspirin, or can you just buy it?
    b. a plan that will make something happen
    > Diet and exercise are a **prescription** for weight loss.
    prescribe *verb* U.S. courts *prescribe* jail terms for some crimes.

15. **preoperative** (prē-ŏp′ər-ə-tĭv; prē-ŏp′rə-tĭv) *adjective* pre- (before) + operate + -ive
    before an operation
    > My **preoperative** requirements included not eating for 24 hours before surgery.

16. **postoperative** (pōst-ŏp′ər-ə-tĭv; pōst-ŏp′rə-tĭv) *adjective* post- (after) + operate + -ive
    after an operation
    > Special **postoperative** nurses <u>monitored</u> the patient after the open heart procedure.

Don't confuse *precede* with *proceed. Proceed* means to move ahead.

prehistoric art

© Pichugin Dmitry/shutterstock.com

Often, *premonitions* involve bad or negative events. However, at times a *premonition* is positive.

17. posterity (pŏst-ĕr'ĭ-tē) *noun*   post- (after) + -ity
    a. the people who will live after you
       The life of Confederate General Robert E. Lee fascinates **posterity.**
    b. all of a person's descendants
       His **posterity** included five children and two grandchildren.

18. posthumous (pŏs'chə-məs) *adjective*   post- (after) + human + -ous
    after death; happening after a person dies
       In his will, he set up a **posthumous** scholarship fund for college students.
    posthumously *adverb*   Ulysses S. Grant wrote his life story while he was
       sick, and it was published *posthumously.*

19. postpone (pōst-pōn') *verb*   post- (after) + ponere (place)
    to delay until a future time
       Since it is raining, we will have to **postpone** our trip to the beach.
    postponement *noun*   We asked the judge for a *postponement* of the trial.

20. postseason (pōst'sē'zən)   post- (after) + season
    a. *noun* the period of time after a season has been completed
       The player's performance in the **postseason** gave us hope that our team
       could win the championship.
    b. *adjective* after a season ends
       The baseball player made the first three-run single in **postseason** history.

DEFINITIONS: Write the correct word for each meaning.

precede	prehistoric	premonition	prescription	preoperative
postoperative	posterity	posthumous	postpone	postseason

_____ 1. to come before

_____ 2. to delay

_____ 3. after an operation

_____ 4. referring to a time before writing

_____ 5. after a season ends

_____ 6. people who live after you

_____ 7. after death

_____ 8. a feeling that something is about to happen

_____ 9. a written order for medicine

_____ 10. before an operation

PART 2 EXERCISES

CONTEXT: ITEMS 1–9: Choose the best answer. **ITEM 10:** Circle true (T) or false (F).

a. precede	b. prehistoric	c. premonition	d. prescription	e. preoperative
f. postoperative	g. posterity	h. posthumous	i. postpone	j. postseason

_____ 1. I would like to ___ my decision until I have more time to think about the matter.

_____ 2. During the ___, the soccer team went over strategies that had worked well.

_____ 3. The marine who had been killed in battle received a ___ medal for bravery.

_____ 4. You need to rest during the ___ period after your appendix is removed.

_____ 5. As I was driving to work, I got a ___ that something was wrong there.

_____ 6. I will consult a doctor to see if I need a ___ for pain medication.

_____ 7. To avoid problems, <u>methodical</u> planning should ___ a camping trip.

_____ 8. Although they didn't write, ___ humans left records through pottery and graves.

_____ 9. Over 2000 years after his death, Julius Caesar is remembered by ___.

T   F   10. *Preoperative* care *precedes* surgery.

DERIVATIONS: Write the correct word form using the choices below.

1. My doctor _____ sleeping pills (**prescribed, prescription**)

2. Can we get a _____ of the due date? (**postpone, postponement**)

3. Please ignore the _____ orders and obey these. (**precedes, preceding**)

4. The star was _____ <u>initiated</u> into the hall of fame. (**posthumous, posthumously**)

FINISH UP: Complete each sentence with a detailed phrase.

5. *Prehistoric* humans _____

_____.

6. During the *postseason*, the basketball player _____

_____.

7. I had a *premonition* that _____

_____.

GIVE EXAMPLES: Answer with personal responses.

8. How would you would like *posterity* to remember you?

9. Whom might you consult to make *preoperative* arrangements?

10. Give an example of *postoperative* instructions to a patient.

PASSAGE: Republic of Baseball

Fill in the word from each column's list that fits best.

Column 1 Choices: bifocals, bilingual, prehistoric, preceded, uniform, unique

Column 2 Choices: posterity, posthumous, postoperative, postseason, premonitions, unison

When major league baseball players are all dressed in the same way, they have a (1) _____ appearance. But they come from many different backgrounds. In fact, the number of foreign-born players in the U.S. has *tripled* in the past twenty years, and the Dominican Republic <u>dominates</u> in producing them.

The Island of Hispaniola, in the Caribbean, is *bisected* into two countries—Haiti and the Dominican Republic. The island has a rich history,

and (2) _____ paintings more than 5,000 years old have been found in caves. Yet, many people there are poor.

It is *universally* agreed that the Dominican Republic is a leader in baseball talent. Since almost ten percent of major leaguers come from the tiny country, it is sometimes called "The Republic of Baseball."

Players are often (3) _____ in English and Spanish, which is spoken in the Dominican Republic. A few, like former San Francisco Giant Daniel Zacapa, are even *trilingual*.

What is special about the Dominican Republic? Many people believe that it has a culture that values baseball. The fact that school lasts only a half day and the desperate wish to escape poverty adds up to a *prescription* for producing dedicated players. Other <u>observers</u> think that physical factors play a part. An analyst writes that boys from the country are

(4) _____ in their flexibility and speed.

Of course, being a great baseball player is

(5) _____ by years of <u>tedious</u> practice—sometimes with broomsticks for bats. At least two players have come from the deepest poverty. Sammy Sosa's father died when he was seven. His

family moved to an abandoned hospital. Perhaps he

had (6) _____ of greatness as he shined shoes and sold oranges to support his family. However, it would have been hard to predict success from his early life.

Miguel Tejada was one of eleven children. Hurricane David destroyed their home. His first glove was made of milk cartons. Tejada's older brother, Juancito, was a great player, but poor medical care for a <u>fracture</u> prevented him becoming a professional.

Athletes who make the majors get better care for their injuries. During the 2008

(7) _____, Albert Pujols received sophisticated surgery on his elbow. Fortunately his

(8) _____ recovery went well. This popular player has been given the Roberto Clemente award for sportsmanship and service.

But not all players are so successful. Thirty-year-old Mario Encamacion was found dead in a Taipei hotel after he had been suspended for taking

steroids. A (9) _____ examination, revealed drugs in his system. As this story shows, there are tremendous pressures on Dominican Republic players. <u>Observers</u> report that the U.S. baseball industry hires these <u>immigrants</u> for much less than they pay U.S.-born players.

Still, players from The Republic of Baseball have played brilliantly and left a wonderful legacy to

Republic of Baseball

© Carlos E. Santa Maria/shutterstock.com

(10) _____.

Think About the Passage

1. Do you think that being *bilingual* in Spanish would help an English-speaking coach? Why?

2. Give two factors that may contribute to the success of Dominican Republic players.

This section will help you review words from lessons 10, 11, and 12. It will also provide practice in the strategy of using prefixes and suffixes.

DEFINITIONS: Fill in the letter that matches the definition of each word.

_____ 1. aimless

_____ 2. unrest

_____ 3. nonflammable

_____ 4. nonrecurring

_____ 5. offender

_____ 6. posthumous

_____ 7. premonition

_____ 8. triple

_____ 9. unison

_____ 10. unsettling

a. not able to burn

b. sung or spoken together

c. not showing up

d. without goals

e. having three parts

f. happening only once

g. a criminal; a person who breaks rules

h. disturbing

i. after death

j. political protest and violence

k. after a season

l. a feeling or hint that something is about to happen

DERIVATIONS: Write the correct word form from the choices below.

1. His _____ got him into trouble. (**noncompliance, compliance, compliances**)

2. We love this _____ vegetable casserole. (**flavorful, flavorless, flavor**)

3. The doctor _____ medicine. (**prescribing, prescribe, prescribed**)

4. A lovely stream _____ the city. (**bisect, bisecting, bisected**)

5. The kind man was _____ loved. (**universe, universally, universal**)

6. He wanted to do the right thing, so he made a(n) _____ decision. (**principle, principled, unprincipled**)

7. Your mother is still crying over the _____ remark that you made. (**tactless, tactful, tact**)

CONTEXT: Write in the letter of the word that best completes each sentence. Use each choice only once

a. bilingual	b. meteorologist	c. nonassertive	d. noninvasive
e. posterity	f. postoperative	g. restless	h. trilingual
i. unbecoming	j. unconventional	k. uniformity	l. unsettling

_____ 1. She was ___ and always seems to do things differently from others.

_____ 2. A(n) ___ person often does not speak very much.

_____ 3. The ___ man twisted in the chair.

_____ 4. Maybe that scarf looks good on someone else, but it is ___ to you.

_____ 5. There was ___ of evaluation because everyone took the same exam.

_____ 6. I am ___ in Greek, Armenian, and English.

_____ 7. The ___ predicted rain from the air-mass movements.

_____ 8. This ___ brain scan will not even touch your body.

_____ 9. Mozart, who lived from 1756 to 1791, left beautiful music for ___.

_____ 10. The ___ staff helps patients who are coming out of surgery.

PASSAGE: A Tiny Horse That Made History

Fill in the word from each column's list that fits best.

Column 1 Choices: biologists, conquerors, nonhazardous, nonstandard, performers, prehistoric, unaccustomed, unfounded

Column 2 Choices: dutifully, flavorful, neglectful, postponed, preceded, spotless, unfounded, unique

The (1) _____ who study animals tell us that the first horses were the size of large dogs.

These (2) _____ animals, who lived almost 35 million years ago, were the ancestors of large modern horses. Some horses living today are also quite small. These miniature horses are not common, however, and you are probably

(3) _____ to seeing them. They

are (4) _____ in size and range from 19 to 38 inches, which is unusually small for a horse.

Throughout history, most people favored large

horses. Ancient (5) _____ wanted powerful horses to drive war chariots. Farmers and travelers needed strong animals to pull plows, drive coaches, and carry people.

But small horses had value too. Children often used them to learn riding skills, for being on a small

horse was a relatively (6) _____ activity, especially when compared with putting a small child on a large horse. Small horses were also bred to work in mines, where they could fit in low, narrow places.

Today, small horses continue to be useful. They

may be bred as (7) _____ to compete in horse shows. They may also be kept as pets, for they are affectionate and good-natured animals.

Miniature horses relieve themselves less frequently than large horses. They can also be trained to make a sign, such as a scratching sound, when they need to go outside to do this.

So a person can keep her house

(8) _____, without fear of an accident.

Miniature horses are also used as guide animals for people with disabilities, including the blind. The horses do not cause allergies, live up to 35 years, and

(9) _____ follow the commands of their owners.

One miniature horse, Midnite, recently made history for receiving an artificial leg. Midnite is the only horse in history to have one, so his case is

(10) _____.

Midnite was born without much of his left hind leg. The original owners were

(11) _____ and did not take care of him. So the sheriff's office gave the horse to the Ranch Hand Rescue organization in Texas. When Midnite arrived, he was so skinny and depressed that the staff was afraid he might die. But their fears were

(12) _____, for he soon gained weight and became friendly.

Workers became fond of Midnite and searched for a way to help him walk normally. Many steps

(13) _____ the receipt of the artificial leg. First, getting the leg was

(14) _____ until Midnite was restored to health; next, the staff showed him how to lie down and rise. After that, the Soft Ride company donated an artificial boot.

Finally the Prostheticare company made the first artificial horse leg. Midnite walked correctly after his first fitting. At his second fitting, to everyone's amazement, Midnite started to run! Today, Midnite runs like a normal horse. He is a tribute to all those who work to rescue animals.

© Zuzule/shutterstock.com

STRATEGY REVIEW: Using prefix, root, and suffix meanings with context clues, fill in the letter of the best choice to complete each sentence.

a. bicarbonate	b. bimetallic	c. blameless	d. instructor
e. noncombatant	f. noncommittal	g. organizer	h. postdate
i. postindustrial	j. premed	k. stressful	l. triangle
m. unilingual	n. unstuck	o. unsubscribe	p. violinist

_____ 1. A(n) ___ is a shape with three angles.

_____ 2. He cannot commit to anything, and is very ___.

_____ 3. A(n) ___ material is made from two metals.

_____ 4. If you don't want to get that newsletter, click on the button to ___.

_____ 5. The ___ student prepared for medical school.

_____ 6. A person who speaks only one language may be called ___.

_____ 7. The teacher of a course may be called a(n) ___.

_____ 8. When you ___ a check, you put a later date on it.

_____ 9. The ___ played in the orchestra.

_____ 10. The soldier was a(n) ___ who was not assigned to fight.

_____ 11. The ___ time refers to the years after factories were started.

_____ 12. I can't get this tape ___ from the wall without damaging the paint.

_____ 13. This ___ activity makes me nervous.

_____ 14. The ___ of the event makes sure everything happens on time.

_____ 15. If it isn't my fault, then I am ___.

EXPANDED GUIDE TO PARTS OF SPEECH

NOUNS: NAMING WORDS

Definition: Person (**Frank**), place (**Hawaii**), thing (**keyboard, Saturday**), idea (**truth**)
The -**ing** forms of verbs can serve as gerunds, which function as nouns: **Walking** is good for you.

ADJECTIVES: DESCRIBING WORDS

Definition: Words that describe nouns or pronouns. Examples: **tired** child; **difficult** test
Attributive nouns: Sometimes a noun can serve as an adjective. Examples: **peer** group;
   patron discounts. (*Peer* and *patron* are nouns that function as adjectives.)
Present and past participles: -**ing** and -**ed** added to verbs can serve as adjectives.
   The following example uses the verb **to bore.**
      Present: (-**ing** form) The **boring** man made us yawn. (The man is *boring* us.)
      Past: (-**ed** form) The **bored** man yawned. (The man is *bored* by other people.)
Adjectives and the verb "to be" (including the words **is, are, were, was, am**)
   Adjectives are often placed after the verb *to be*: The stove is **hot**; She is **bored**.
   The adjectives (**hot, bored**) describe nouns that are subjects of the sentence (**stove, man**).
Comparatives, Superlatives:
      One-syllable words: add -*er*, -*est*; if word ends in *e* add -*r*, -*st*: **tall, taller, tallest; wide,**
      wider, widest.
      Two-syllable words ending with *y*: change *y* to *i*, add -*er*, -*est*: **merry, merrier, merriest.**
      Other words of 2 or more syllables: use **more** and **most**: **more intelligent; most intelligent**.
Articles: These are the words **a, an,** and **the.** They describe nouns. The word **a** is used
   before words starting with consonant sounds; **an** is used (instead of **a**) before vowel
   sounds. Examples: **a** tree; **an** apple

ADVERBS: DESCRIBING WORDS

Definition: Words that describe verbs, adjectives, or other adverbs.
Note: Many adverbs are formed by adding -*ly* to an adjective: **Extreme** (adjective);
   extremely (adverb)
   He walks **slowly**. (*Slowly* describes the verb *walks*.)
   He was an **extremely** tired child. (*Extremely* describes the adjective *tired*.)
   He walked **very** slowly to school. (*Very* describes the adverb *slowly*.)

VERBS: ACTION AND STATE WORDS

Definition: Words that express an action or a state of being.
Notes: The verb **"to be"** usually expresses a state of being.
   The *infinitive* form of a verb is that verb preceded by "to," as in **to hurry** and **to waste**.
   Many common verbs are irregular. These include **to be, to go, to come, to see, to say.**
Transitive and intransitive verbs:
   A *transitive* verb has a direct object: I **saw** a dog. (The direct object is *dog*.)
   An *intransitive* verb does NOT have a direct object: I **walked**; I **walked** to the store.
   A direct object tells *what* or *who*. It does NOT have a preposition (such as "to") before it.
Common verb tenses:
   Present tense: In regular verbs, add an -*s* only to the third person singular verb form.

	Singular	*Plural*
First Person	I walk.	We walk.
Second Person	You walk.	You walk. (*You* is more than one person.)
Third Person	He, she, it walks.	They walk.

Present progressive tense: This is formed by the verb **to be** and the **-ing** form (or present participle) of another verb. It refers to an action started in the past that is still going on. Examples: I **am walking**. He **is walking**.

Simple past tense: In regular verbs, add an *-ed* to form the past tense: He **walked**.

Simple future tense: The word **will** put in front of a verb forms a future tense: I **will** walk.

Progressive future tense: The verb **to be** plus **going to** forms the progressive future tense. This often means "very soon." They **are going to** walk; I **am going to** walk.

Forms with *-ing* and *-ed*: (These have already been referred to above.)
Adding *-ing* to a verb yields a present participle or a gerund: **walking, boring**
Adding *-ed* to a verb yields a past participle: **walked, bored**

Active and Passive Voices: In an active voice the subject of a sentence is put first. In a passive voice, the subject of a sentence is the object of the action. Below, the object of action is **dog.**
Active Voice: Ted **walked** the dog.
Passive Voice: The dog **was walked** by Ted.

PRONOUNS: REPLACEMENTS FOR NOUNS

Pronouns replace a noun. Example pronouns: **he, she, we, us, they, it.**
Example sentences:
Noun used: **John** walked.
Pronoun used: **He** walked.

CONJUNCTIONS: CONNECTOR WORDS

Conjunctions connect words, phrases, or clauses.
Examples of conjunctions: **and, but, yet, for so, although, nor, because, however.**
Example sentences: We sell meat **and** fruit. We went, **but** he stayed.

INTERJECTIONS: EMOTION AND INSERTED WORDS, PHRASES

These words or phrases express emotion or make insertions.
Interjection examples: **Ouch! Really great! Um,** yes.

PREPOSITIONS: CONNECTING A PHRASE

These join words to phrase in a sentence. Example: I go **to** the store. The preposition **to** joins the phrase **the store** to the sentence. The words **to the store** form a *prepositional phrase.*
Examples of prepositions: **about, above, across, after, against, at, before, behind, below, beside, by, for, from, in, inside, into, of, off, on, out, over, through, to, toward, under, until, up, with.**

SOME COMPLEX VERB TENSES:

Progressive tenses: These are formed with **to be** and the present participle **-ing.** The progressive tense often describes unfinished events or events that continue for a while.
Present progressive: Examples: I **am walking**. (This is described above.)
Past progressive: I **was talking** when she called.
Future progressive: I **will be walking** on the trip. (This is described above.)

Perfect tenses: These are formed with **to have** and the past participle **-ed.** The perfect tense often describes actions that have been completed, or are expected to be completed.
Present perfect: Examples: I **have finished** my paper.
Past perfect: I **had walked** when he arrived. (Walking was finished before he arrived.)
Future perfect: I **will have walked** by the time he arrives. (Walking will be finished by the time he arrives.)

This explanation of a dictionary entry uses the example entry **rule** as a reference.

a. **Entry Word:** Given in bold. (See line 1 in the entry below.)

b. **Pronunciation:** Given in parentheses (line 1). The key is given in a dictionary, or there is a pronunciation key on the front, inside cover of this book.

c. **Part of Speech:** Here are some common abbreviations:
   n. – noun   *tr. v.* – transitive verb   *intr. v.* – intransitive verb
   adj. – adjective   *adv.* – adverb

   Some words are many parts of speech. Rule is a *n* (line 1), *tr. v.* (line 13), and *intr.v.* (line 17) Entries often give word forms. Nouns give irregular plurals. Adjectives give comparatives (*er, est*). Verbs give past tense (which is also the past participle), present participle, and third person singular present tense form (line 13). Verb forms may be given without the first syllable (for *answer: -swered, -swering, -swers*).

d. **Definitions:**
   Related definitions may be divided into parts a and b. (lines 1–2, 16).
   Some definitions are used in special fields: lines 7, *Mathematics*; 9, *Law*; 11, *Printing*.
   Definitions may have usage labels, like *Slang* (see line 20), *Informal* (not accepted in formal speech), *Obs.* (for "obsolete," no longer used), or *Archaic* (no longer used).
   Phrasal verbs and idioms are phrases, with special meanings, containing the word (lines 21, 22). Words may be marked that show you where to find synonyms for this entry word (see line 16).

e. **Etymology:** This is the history of a word (line 23), with the oldest form last. Abbreviations for etymology include ME (Middle English); OE (Old English); L (Latin); VLat (Vulgar Latin, nonstandard); F (French); OF (Old French); G (Greek from 2500 years ago).

f. **Related Words:** These are words formed from an entry word. They are other parts of speech. *Rule* has the related word *rulable*, an adjective (lines 23–24).

(1)	**rule** (rool) *n.* **1a.** Governing power or its possession or use; authority. **b.** The duration of such power. **2a.** An authoritative prescribed direction for conduct. **b.** The body of regulations prescribed by the founder of a religious order for governing
(5)	the conduct of its members. **3.** A usual, customary, or generalized course of action or behavior. **4.** A generalized statement that describes what is true in most or all cases. **5.** *Mathematics* A standard method or procedure for solving a class of problems. **6.** *Law* **a.** A court order limited in application to a specific case.
(10)	**b.** A subordinate regulation governing a particular matter. **7.** See **ruler** 2. **8.** *Printing* A thin metal strip of various widths and designs, used to print borders or lines, as between columns. ❖ *v.* **ruled, rul•ing, rules**—*tr.* **1.** To exercise control, dominion, or direction over; govern. **2.** To dominate by powerful
(15)	influence. **3.** To decide or declare authoritatively or judicially; decree. See Syns at **decide. 4a.** To mark with straight parallel lines. **b.** To mark (a straight line), as with a ruler. —*intr.* **1.** To be in total control or command; exercise supreme authority. **2.** To formulate and issue a decree or decision. **3.** To prevail at
(20)	a particular level or rate. **4.** *Slang* To be excellent or superior: *That new movie rules!* —*phrasal verb:* **rule out 1.** To prevent; preclude. **2.** To remove from consideration; exclude. —*idiom:* **as a rule** In general; for the most part. [ME *reule* < OFr. < VLat. *regula* < Lat. *rēgula*, rod, principle.] —**rul′a•ble** *adj.*

INDEX